The Universe
Next Door

The Universe Next Door

A PERSONAL ODYSSEY

Judith Hemenway

BEST PUBLISHING COMPANY

Design by: Jill McAdoo
Edited by: Rebekah Guzman

International Standard Book Number: 1-930536-20-8
Library of Congress Control Number: 2003111364

For more information contact:
Best Publishing Company
2355 North Steves Boulevard
P.O. Box 30100
Flagstaff, AZ 86003-0100 USA
Tele: 928.527.1055
Fax: 928.526.0370
divebooks@bestpub.com
www.bestpub.com

Contents

Perspective

You study the Self
Or the Universe. I say:
Sun and Cheek kissing.

Dedication

For my father, who cherished and nurtured my will to explore,
For my mother, whose love of nature's beauty lives on in me.

For Virden Bryan, who taught me how to dive so many years ago,
For Brenda Ellis, George Ames, Don Casey, Bill Proud, Pete
Greenwood, Paul Doose, and Steve Wilson,
who dive now in the Infinite Blue,
And for all the other Blue Fins still living, with whom
I have shared so many wonderful adventures.

For Dr. Herbert Tanney, who saved my life,
and Dr. Jeffrey Sandler, who keeps me functioning.

For Patti Metz, Joe Hlebica, and Kim Harlow,
who have helped me find my voice,
And most of all for my husband: respected colleague, best friend,
and soul mate, whose love warms and fills my universe.

Foreword

A LOVE SONG TO THE SEA

Thirty years ago, two strangers made a life-defining decision—they took up scuba diving. Neither one of them realized the enormity of what they'd done; that only became apparent as the decades passed. A few months after they became certified divers, these two strangers joined the Santa Monica Blue Fins diving club. Lightning didn't strike them then either, but this was also a significant event.

The two strangers were Judy Hemenway and myself, Bonnie J. Cardone. Diving, the sport we took up so casually—me, by myself, and Judy, with her husband, Jon—soon became the center of our lives. We've met some of our dearest friends through diving, most especially through the Blue Fins. We've had our greatest and most hilarious adventures on dive trips, many of them also with the Fins.

In our decades of diving, Judy and I have learned an incredible amount about the sea, its inhabitants, and ourselves. We wanted to share our fun and adventures with others as well as pass on the wisdom we've gathered. Judy is doing that with this book. You might call it her love song to the sea and to divers everywhere.

Bonnie J. Cardone

Bonnie J. Cardone was an editor/writer/photographer for Skin Diver Magazine for 22 years, with more than 900 articles to her credit. She is also the author of several books. Bonnie was named Woman Diver of the Year in 1999 and was one of the first women inducted into the Women Divers Hall of Fame.

Introduction

With me it is an imperative, as fundamental and organic as breathing: I must have contact with the natural world. Frequently, intensely, personally.

For 30 years now, five days a week, I have traveled in my enclosed car through the urban streets of Southern California to my climate-controlled office. Frequently, I work behind cipher-locked doors, in windowless rooms filled with the hum and heat of the computers and cables that are the focus of my efforts. Being a security engineer and systems analyst, I rarely deal with the physical machines themselves. My world is that of the mind, the abstract: programs, protocols, applications, theories, models, virtual machines, virtual memory, and virtual reality. These are concepts which float disembodied, far removed from the physical mother-boards and memory chips of the machines.

In such an environment, physical reality becomes warped beyond recognition. There is no day or night, nor are there seasons. Time is measured in nanoseconds and each nanosecond is the same as all the others. Schedule pressure is intense: The explosion of technological advances and the heat of competition in the marketplace provide a pressure cooker of an environment. Trying to keep pace, my husband says, is like drinking from a fire hose. It is exciting, challenging, exasperating, exhausting, rewarding, and fulfilling. And woefully incomplete.

In 1948, two years after I was born, a cousin of Jacques Cousteau named Rene Bussoz sold the first Aqua Lungs in the United States from his new dive shop near the UCLA campus. That same year, medical researcher Edward Kendall synthesized Cortisone for the first time. The Cortisone has saved my life and the Aqua Lung has enriched it beyond measure.

Three years after I attained my scuba certification, I was diagnosed with Addison's disease, which causes the body's immune system to destroy the adrenal glands. Without treatment, it is invariably fatal. The primary treatment is Cortisone. Seven years later, I was diagnosed with a second auto-immune disorder which destroyed my thyroid glands. A year after that, I began showing symptoms of Chronic Fatigue Immune Deficiency Syndrome. Most recently I was diagnosed with Sjogren's Syndrome, which causes destruction of the salivary glands and tear ducts and is frequently accompanied by fatigue and generalized tissue inflammation. My doctors tell me that I may develop additional auto-immune disorders in the future. There are no cures for any of them.

The ancient Greeks had the right idea: a sound mind in a sound body. A balance of the mental and the physical. Over the years, I have found many ways to maintain this balance: In addition to taking my Cortisone and other medications faithfully, I exercise regularly, eat healthy, work in my garden, walk on the beach, and go camping in our nearby deserts and mountains. But more than anything else, my balance comes from the ocean.

Having grown up during the 50s, when scuba diving was a manly enterprise, the domain of Navy Seals and heroes such as Mike Nelson of TV-land's Sea Hunt, I was 27-years-old before it occurred to me that I, a mere female, could become a diver. This insight came to me during my first conversation with the man who was to become my husband and partner in life's adventures. All I needed to do, he said, was to take a six-week course at the local YMCA. I had been planning on going back to graduate school for my doctorate; I'd been accepted into the program at UCLA and had money set aside for tuition. After carefully considering the alternatives, I chose the scuba course instead, using my tuition money to buy all the paraphernalia that humans require in order to survive underwater. Two months later, in October of 1973, I became a certified scuba diver. I've never regretted that choice.

The ocean really is another Universe: separate, distinct, exotic, and foreign. As air-breathing mammals, we cannot survive within it for more than a few precious moments. Although we evolved from the ocean and are ourselves composed largely of water, our evolution has condemned us to skimming the surface.

Swimming, surfing, sailing, and motoring, we frolic at its fringes and race across its vast expanse, completely oblivious to the universe beneath us. From the first moment I immersed my mask-protected head into the waters off Catalina Island, I was gripped by an intense and undeniable urge to explore that universe. Over the 30 years since then, I have dived countless times, in the waters of Southern California, the Caribbean, and the South Pacific. These experiences have kept me sane and healthy, nurturing my body and spirit as nothing else can. In the following pages, I offer you a hint of what the universe of the ocean contains. Mere words cannot convey the full reality of such a place—they can only sketch and approximate. I write in the hope that my approximations will also entertain and inspire.

> *pity this busy monster, manunkind,*
>
> *not. Progress is a comfortable disease:*
> *your victim(death and life safely beyond)*
>
> *plays with the bigness of his littleness*
> *-electrons deify one razorblade*
> *into a mountainrange;lenses extend*
>
> *unwish through curving wherewhen til unwish*
> *returns on its unself.*
> *A world of made*
> *is not a world of born - pity poor flesh*
>
> *and trees, poor stars and stones, but never this*
> *fine specimen of hypermagical*
>
> *ultraomnipotence. We doctors know*
>
> *a hopeless case if - listen:there's a hell*
> *of a good universe next door;let's go*
>
> *– E.E. Cummings*

Flying

Delicious freedom—
To glide and soar unfettered,
Weightless in deep blue.

Flying

As a scuba diver, one of the first lessons I had to learn about the ocean was that it is bigger than I am—much, much bigger—and infinitely more powerful. Novice divers are notorious for gulping down their air supply in record time and I was certainly no exception. Every time I entered the water, I was tense, excited, and jazzed to a jangling frenzy by the excess adrenalin coursing through my veins. Instinctively, I fought to stay on the surface with my head out of the water, even though I had a regulator that reliably and steadily delivered air to my lungs. I also fought to stay in one place as the water undulated and surged and slapped, moving me wherever and whenever it chose. It took several months before the lesson began to sink in: It is useless to argue with the ocean. In any contest between a human and the ocean, the ocean will always win. Always. The only option I have in the matter is whether I choose to want what the ocean wants. So choosing allows me the silly little illusion that I am in control and doing what I want to do. Once I began to get the hang of this particular flavor of self-delusion, diving became a delightful game.

Near the end of my first winter of diving, Jon and I were busy practicing this game at a spot called Cortes Banks. Cortes is a shallow reef structure located about 80 miles due west of the U.S.-Mexican border. There are one or two spots on the reef that are shallow enough to warrant a marker buoy, but nowhere does the reef break the surface. Sitting on a dive boat anchored at Cortes, one can scan the horizon for a full 360 degrees and not see any land. The reef has long been an extremely productive fishing spot, for both fish and lobster, and hence is worth the arduous 8–10 hour boat ride from San Pedro harbor. Because the site is unprotected by any landmass, conditions here are frequently quite rough, with long powerful ground swells, sometimes topped with wind-driven chop like icing on a cake.

Such were the conditions on this particular day. It was near the end of lobster season, so we elected to stay and do at least one, possibly two, dives here in spite of the conditions, before heading east to the protection of San Clemente Island. We were diving the Nine-Fathom spot, one of the shallow areas with a marker buoy. We managed to suit up on the rocking, pitching deck without injuring either ourselves or others, which is a real challenge given the 100-plus pounds of gear required to do cold-water diving like this! We even managed to get ourselves overboard into the rolling, choppy waters and made our way with as much haste as possible to the bottom, where we hoped the conditions would be more serene.

Now, what you must understand is that the up-and-down swell action of the ocean surface is translated into a back-and-forth surge action for some depth beneath the surface, the depth depending on the height of the surface swell. If you can dive deep enough, you can get beneath this surge into still, calm waters. On this day, at this spot, the bottom was at 60 feet, which wasn't deep enough.

We set a compass heading for the direction we wanted to travel and began kicking, scanning the reef beneath us as we went, searching for the tell-tale antennae of our intended prey—the spiny lobsters. As we headed into the surge, I realized that I had to kick as hard as I possibly could just to stay in one spot—at least until the surge changed from forth to back, at which point I was carried along quite handily. I quickly realized that I would exhaust myself within a few rounds of fighting. I took a deep breath and recalled my recently learned lesson: Don't argue with the ocean. The next time the surge changed and moved in the wrong direction, I grabbed hold of a sturdy piece of kelp and held tight. Flapping in the "breeze," I waited for the surge to again turn in my favor, at which point I kicked like hell and zoomed at a dizzying speed across the reef. What a marvelous game! I looked to my left to see Jon doing exactly the same thing. We continued this diversion for about 15 minutes, alternately flapping and zooming. It was such fun that I almost forgot about looking for "bugs" (diver-speak for lobsters). The act of moving through the ocean had ceased to be a means to an end and had become an end in itself—a tandem joyride in unison with the water.

Abruptly, on one of our forward zooms, the world fell out from under me. The entire reef disappeared in an instant. My heart leaped into my throat, my stomach flipped over twice, and my semi-circular canals went completely haywire. I was flying through deep blue space unbounded. Ahead, above, below, on either side, there was nothing visible but an intense and infinite dark blue expanse. The sensation of flying, of moving rapidly and weightlessly through space, was intoxicating! And disorienting. Without any reference points whatsoever, it was hard to tell how fast I was going, or even in what direction. I looked back and saw the drop-off of the reef rapidly flying forward to greet me. Jon was nearby, suspended over the abyss like myself. Reassured, we spent a few moments soaring back and forth, immersing ourselves in the sheer exuberance of flight, before reluctantly agreeing that it was time to begin working our way back toward the boat, reversing our charted compass course.

Several months later, while on our honeymoon in Cozumel, the memory of that soaring flight at Cortes came flashing back to me as I swam away from Palancar reef toward the island. I was in about 50 feet of crystal clear water with sunlight dancing in networks of shimmering ribbons across a vast expanse of white sand. I was weightless and, in the warm tropical waters, unencumbered by the awkward restrictions of a wetsuit. The urge that seized me was irresistible: I spread my arms out at my sides and, kicking furiously, I soared and looped, reeled and rolled in three-dimensional space, doing a perfect child's imitation of a barnstorming biplane. It was a delicious, exuberant feeling of pure abandonment; I was in love, and I was free, and I was flying.

The Snail

Oh lucky creature——
Proudly carrying aloft
Your own treasure chest.

The Jewel

I might have known that it would not be a normal evening. After all, the place was called Los Locos, which means "The Crazy Ones." For a little bar in a tiny Mexican fishing village, it was unexpectedly teeming with noisy patrons, both Mexican and American. A small mariachi band wandered around the room, playing their infectious tunes, smiling and nodding at everyone.

"I'd like one of those, please," Jon said, pointing to the large bright yellow piece of paper tacked up next to the mirror behind the bar. A white hand-printed price tag announced that the paper cost $2.00. The bartender, a scruffy-looking ex-pat American named Larry with long, stringy brown hair and a forest of bushy brown beard, gave Jon a sly sideways grin and replied, "It comes with a ceremony, you know." Jon looked at me, his face a mixture of amusement and challenge and question, and then said to the bartender, "That'll be fine," as he handed over the requisite two dollars.

With lightening speed, our host retrieved one of the precious yellow papers from under the bar and laid it before us, along with a pen. We dutifully filled out the form as required. In large bold letters, the paper declared itself to be an **8-Hour Marriage License**:

> BE IT KNOWN THAT ON THIS DAY [FILL IN THE DATE HERE] IN THE LOVER'S PARADISE KNOWN AS LA BUFADORA, THAT [GROOM'S NAME HERE] AND [BRIDE'S NAME HERE], HE BEING THE GROOM, AND A NOBLE-HEARTED MAN ENCASED IN VIRTUE'S ARMOUR, AND SHE BEING THE BRIDE, AND A FROLICSOME MAIDEN FAIR AS YOUNG MORNING, DID SOLEMNLY ENTER INTO UNHOLY MATRIMONY FOR A PERIOD OF 8 HOURS, AND ARE COMPLETELY FREE, FOR SAID 8

HOURS, TO AVIDLY AND LOVINGLY SAMPLE THE DELICIOUS MORSELS OF A TRUE AND HONORABLE RUNAWAY COUPLE'S PASSIONATE HONEYMOON.

At the bottom, in fine print, was the note,

"THIS LICENSE IS TRANSFERABLE."

As soon as we had completed the form, Larry shouted to gather everyone around, announcing that there was to be a wedding immediately. A great cheer rose up, as Larry's Mexican partner solemnly approached us carrying a thick book covered in black leather. From somewhere deep within the crowd, a very colorful piece of a broken papier mache piñata appeared: it was the head of a rooster, which I was to hold as my bridal bouquet. I laughed aloud at the thinly disguised symbolism. Obviously, this particular version of the wedding ceremony had been done here before. As Larry retrieved the book from his partner and opened it to begin the ceremony, it was Jon's turn to laugh: being an engineer, he immediately recognized the CRC Handbook, a reference book of engineering tables published by the Chemical Rubber Company. The contents of the book did not, however, deter our hosts from giving us a very reasonable facsimile of a real wedding ceremony—or at least the English version was a reasonable facsimile. I have no idea what it was that his partner was saying in Spanish. But every time he paused and looked at us, we said "si" and he would smile and nod and continue. A couple of paper cigar bands served as our rings and within a very short time, we were pronounced husband and wife. We kissed enthusiastically as the crowd cheered and the mariachi band broke into more of their exuberant songs. The beer flowed and the band played and we danced away the hours in a joyful celebration.

After spending the eight hours of our passionate honeymoon snuggled chastely in separate sleeping bags in a tent with three of our best friends, we fortified ourselves with huevos rancheros at the local restaurant, Dos Tortugas (The Two Turtles), and went out to hire a local fisherman for our first dive. The three of us who were diving piled our gear into his panga and he rowed us out across the little bay around the rocky point to a pinnacle called White Rock, which sits as a sentinel for La Bufadora (The Blowhole). This spectacular natural phenomenon is caused by waves as they're funneled into a large V-shaped inlet that slices deeply into the high cliffs. The force of the channeled waves creates a loud roar as the water leaps in a great hissing white plume 40–50 feet into the air. We would have to be more than "loco" to dive within the churning inlet, but the waters around White Rock were relatively calm.

Using a combination of gestures and broken English, the fisherman indicated that he would follow our bubbles as we dived so we didn't have to worry about finding the small (and anchorless) boat when we surfaced—he would find us. With that assurance, we entered the water and began our descent. The water was clear and bracingly cold. Sunlight and shadow played across the rock wall as we drifted slowly down along its face, tracing a zigzag pattern as the surging action of the waves pushed us back and forth. At about 85 feet we added some air to our buoyancy vests to stop our descent and began working back up the wall. If my mouth hadn't been stuffed full of a regulator mouthpiece, I would have been gaping and gawking like a country hick on her first visit to the city. The wall was an explosion of riotous color, packed solid with the yellows and oranges of encrusting sponges and the reds and pinks and purples of the tiny colonial anemones called corynactis, or strawberry anemones. Scattered among them were the smooth brown and white shells of chestnut cowries. Diminutive gobies darted and dashed about, but unlike their drab white northern cousins, these southerners were painted a bright orange-red, with neon blue stripes. I had been diving for less than six months and I had never seen such a beautiful display of life. It echoed the vitality and color of the local Mexican culture that I loved so much.

As we neared the surface, I noticed something tucked in among the anemones and I moved in for a closer examination. It was a cone-shaped top shell, no more than half an inch high. I had seen much larger top shells before, but what was so extraordinary about this one was its colors. The snail-owner of the shell was orange with dark brown spots, and the shell itself was ringed with spiraling beaded bands of purple and gold. This exquisite creature is aptly named the jeweled top shell. There were dozens of them on this wall, adding their sparkling touches to an already gorgeous rockscape. It was the crowning touch to a wonderful dive.

We surfaced about 30 yards further out toward the point than where we had entered the water, but our fisherman and his panga were right there as he had promised. His skillful oar-work kept the boat steady while we clambered back on board and then he rowed us back into the bay to the narrow sandy beach at the base of the cliffs where our non-diving friends awaited us.

That evening after dinner, we gathered around the fireplace in the spacious lounge area of Dos Tortugas. Locals and Americans mingled together, relaxing in the warm flickering light of the fire, sipping beers and chatting amicably. The smell of hot lard and corn tortillas blended with the smoky atmosphere. Ed pulled out his guitar and began to play some folksongs. I sat quietly watching the sunset burnish the hills where dozens of agaves, the ones the locals call Our Lord's Candles, offered up their creamy white blossom clusters to the emerging stars. I looked at Jon as he gently teased two Mexican toddlers who were apparently completely captivated by him. I knew that in five months we'd be replacing our cigar-band rings with gold ones in a real wedding, and I smiled contently. Jon had asked me if I wanted a diamond engagement ring and I had said "no." It made no sense to me to spend huge sums of money on a tiny chunk of carbon when we could spend that money on a diving honeymoon in Cozumel. Besides, on this day, I'd found the only jewel I'd ever need, and I was immensely happy.

Breathless

The sea lies breathless
Molten, thick and glistening:
Heavy with desire.

The Deep

Weightless at 65 feet, we drifted with the current as it flowed along the sheer face of the underwater mountain, moving us southward toward Barracuda Point. I was enchanted by the wealth of corals and schools of fish that moved slowly and leisurely past us, like the reeling backdrop of a low-budget Hollywood movie. But as we closed on the Point, I forced myself to focus on our movements rather than on the beauty of the reef. We had been warned about the Point, about the strong current that usually ran there. My senses went to "alert" status, seeking any hint of change in the flow of the water that carried us. The danger of the current at the Point was that it flowed downward along the flank of the mountain, a vertical wall which plunged 2,000 feet to the ocean floor. An unwary diver could get caught in such a downdraft and, if the current was strong, could be carried swiftly down into the deep. Such currents can kill.

Up ahead, I could see the shallow valley that cut across the end of the Point. The Divemaster had said we must move up and across that valley, rather than going out around the Point, in order to avoid the current.

We were still about 10 feet away from the valley when I felt the water begin to tug gently downward on my body. Ahead of us, I saw our friends Bill and Joann descending rapidly, but before I had time to form a worry in my mind, the current became an insistent force, trying to drag me down to join them. I began kicking and angled up toward the valley, but realized quickly that I was making no progress. I escalated my efforts, throwing every bit of energy and strength I had into my kick and slowly began inching upward. Beside me, Jon was moving more rapidly, his large powerful legs more than a match for the current. At this point, I changed tactics and moved into the reef wall, where I could use my arms to hang on and to help pull me up. I kicked and clawed the remaining 9 feet, at last fighting my way out of the downdraft and into the calm waters of the valley. As I paused to catch my breath and re-orient myself, I looked around to make sure that Jon had made it too. He had and we each blew a kiss to the other in relief and triumph.

Ahead, the others in our group were pausing to do some sight-seeing in the valley: There were about a dozen 3–4-foot white-tipped reef sharks lolling about, a perfect "photo-op" for those with cameras. With a shock, I realized that Bill and Joann were not with us, and then I remembered seeing them heading down the mountain. As I finned over to the Divemaster to alert her to the problem, Bill and Joann came crawling laboriously up into the valley. I quickly formed the hand signal that means, "Are you okay?" They nodded and signed back, "Yes, we're okay." Later, after the dive, they told us the current had dragged them down to 140 feet before they realized what had happened. It was a terribly difficult struggle for them to work their way back up to the safety of the valley, but they had succeeded and, although quite tired, they were otherwise fine.

They were very lucky. The safe limit for scuba diving is 130 to 160 feet. At 132 feet, a human body is subjected to five atmospheres of pressure. At this pressure, large amounts of nitrogen dissolve in the blood, causing a kind of mental confusion called "nitrogen narcosis," or "rapture of the deep."

The first time I experienced this was on a reef in Fiji. This particular reef had a "chimney" in it—a large open hole that plunged straight down 200 feet into the reef. The Divemaster had explained that there were two passageways leading from the inside of the chimney to the outside wall of the reef; the first of these was at 90 feet and the other was at 140 feet. We didn't want to risk going to 140 feet, so our plan was to descend to 90 feet, follow that passageway out of the hole, and then work our way back up the outside wall of the reef.

Four of us began our descent together. The water was crystal clear, intensely blue, and soothingly warm. We sank slowly and languidly, pirouetting as we dropped so that the walls of the hole spiraled around us. It was beautiful and mesmerizing. I searched for a sign of the passageway, but before I spotted it, I noticed that Vicki was waving her hand at me, then pointing to her gauges, and then pointing to me. My mind moved slowly, as though in a thick fog, and I worked on the puzzle for what seemed like hours before I realized that she wanted me to look at my depth gauge. In slow motion I lifted the gauge and stared at its face, trying to decipher the curious markings on it.

I finally focused and realized with a jolt that I was at 110 feet and sinking rapidly. I began to panic and renewed my efforts to search for a passageway out. It did not occur to my muddled mind that we could just begin our ascent immediately and look for the 90-foot passageway. Apparently, it didn't occur to any of my companions either. Jack was pointing downward to where the 140-foot passageway was visible and we all moved toward it, four zombies in slow motion. The passage was large enough to swim through comfortably and short enough that we could see the open ocean beyond. In a few moments we were all on the outside of the wall, working our way slowly upward. At about 90 feet, the fog in my mind began to clear and I realized just how stupid we had been.

The longer a diver remains at depth, the more nitrogen dissolves in the blood. Then, when the diver ascends and the pressure decreases, this dissolved nitrogen converts back to a gas, forming bubbles in the blood—a phenomenon that is very similar to what happens when you pop the top off a bottle of cola. If the diver ascends too far too fast, the nitrogen bubbles that form can be large, perhaps large enough to lodge in a narrow blood vessel somewhere in the body, causing symptoms that range from slight tingling or rashes to sharp pain, dizziness, weakness, and even paralysis and death. This is called decompression sickness, or "the bends." Because of these dangers, sport divers comply with strict time limits, which become shorter the deeper one goes. At 60 feet, the time limit is 60 minutes. At 130 feet, it is less than 5 minutes.

As we ascended the outside wall I checked my dive computer, which indicated that the entire dive thus far had been less than four minutes. But that was awfully close to 5 minutes and we had been at 140 feet. We had not planned for a decompression dive, but we realized that to be safe, we needed to do that now. We continued our slow ascent up to 30 feet, stayed at that depth for 15 minutes and then did a similar stop for 10 minutes at 20 feet before finally rising to the surface. This process of ascending slowly, with a series of timed stops along the way, allows the nitrogen in the blood to "outgas" very slowly in very small bubbles, significantly reducing the chances of getting "bent." We were all very lucky—none of us developed any symptoms of the bends, in spite of our stupidity. How much different it would have been if one of us had gotten stuck in that passageway. Even if the unlucky one had managed to get free, it would have significantly lengthened our time at depth, increasing our chances of getting bent.

Several years after the incident in the chimney, I did get stuck at depth. Jon and I were diving on Farnsworth Bank, a deep reef just off of Catalina Island. We were cruising along at 130 feet enjoying the beauty of the rare purple hydrocoral that grows there when I realized that I was staying in one spot in spite of my finning. Puzzled, I stopped and twisted around to look upward, quickly discovering that I had swam underneath an overhanging ledge with an abandoned fishing net draped over it. Apparently the valve of my scuba tank had snagged the net and I could not reach behind me to clear the tangle. I looked for Jon and saw him 20 feet ahead of me, browsing among the corals. I waved but he didn't see me, so I turned on my underwater lantern, which throws a large and powerful beam. By flashing this light toward him I was able to attract his attention and he came at once to free me. By then we knew we had run out of time, so we began our slow ascent.

It wasn't until we had reached the surface that the panic hit me and I began to hyperventilate and shake, realizing what a close call it had been. If Jon had not noticed my light, I would have had to abandon my tank and do a free ascent 130 feet to the surface. Or, if the net had been so tightly tangled that he couldn't free me, we would have had to "buddy breathe," sharing his regulator and air all the way to the surface. We had been trained to do such feats, but had never had to do them from such a great depth. If I had panicked down there, I probably would have died. That incident was very educational. I learned that I was able to meet a life-threatening emergency head-on, without panic. We both learned that carrying a sharp knife was a really good idea and that equipping our regulators with dual mouthpieces (called an "octopus rig") was a *great* idea.

It is experiences such as these that have taught both of us an enormous respect for the ocean. To immerse oneself in its depths is to experience both its beauty and its danger. By learning from our mistakes and modifying our equipment and behavior, we have been able to minimize the dangers and enjoy many years of diving adventure in the Deep.

Dirty Jack and the Fins

The glowering gray clouds pressed low over the tiny boat as it drifted helplessly in an endless sea. The two lone figures in the boat were struggling with their dive gear and grumbling at each other when—abruptly—the threatening clouds parted and an enormous shaft of radiant golden sunshine streamed forth, sparking fiery reflections on the surface of the sea a few yards from the boat. Oblivious to this remarkable scene, the two divers continued their struggles.

"Dammit, Jack, I can't find the other rubber for my speargun—did you steal it again?"

"Steal it??!!!" Jack exclaimed. "Don't blame me for your screw-ups, Evan! You're the one who can't find his own mouth with a bottle of scotch!"

The bickering continued for several minutes until a disembodied voice boomed out, "Shut up, you idiots, and look around you!"

Jack and Evan stood bolt upright and stared at each other, mouths agape.

"Did you just say something?" Jack asked.

"No. No, Jack, I didn't say a word. What's going …"

The booming voice interrupted the question. "I said, shut up, and look around you!"

In unison, the two men snapped their mouths shut and stared at each other, their eyes wide and startled. Then slowly, as if they were afraid to move too rapidly, they looked around.

"Well, I'll be horn-swoggled," exclaimed Jack as he focused on the patch of shimmering golden water off the port side. There, in the middle of all that radiance, floated an object. Jack dove into the water and swam over for a closer look. Evan could hear Jack's laughter as he reached the object. Jack swam awkwardly back to the boat, towing the thing as though he were rescuing a drowning swimmer. He handed it carefully up to Evan and then clambered back into the boat himself.

The two men sat and contemplated this strange gift from the sea. There before them was an immaculate, finely finished walnut plaque on which was mounted a magnificent set of genuine Texas Longhorns, their symmetric, smooth ivory surfaces spreading gracefully from the central mount, the two polished tips a full six feet apart.

Once more the voice spoke. "You two certainly deserve this. Use it wisely or I'll track you down like miserable curs and kick you into oblivion." With that, the voice and the radiant beam of light were gone. Silently, the two men floated in their tiny boat on the vast sea, staring at the gift bestowed upon them.

And that, dear friends, is how the David–Daniels Bullshit Award was established. Or at least that is how my friend Jack Daniels, a.k.a. Dirty Jack, tells the story. This plaque became the most coveted and sought-after trophy ever awarded to members of our dive club, the Santa Monica Blue Fins. Every year, this prize was inflicted on the member who best exemplified the club's time-honored traditions of Tall Tales, Fish Stories, and other outstanding feats of Truth Stretching. Here's a sampling of the long list of illustrious winners of this coveted award:

Brenda Ellis, Official Dive Mamma and editor of the club newsletter, The Porpoise: The year that she won, Brenda published a special edition of The Porpoise, which she sent every month to Dirty Jack. This special edition indicated that someone other than Jack was leading in the annual spearfishing competition. All the other copies of the newsletter, sent to everyone else in the club, contained the true competition statistics, with Jack in the lead. Thus, Jack had no idea that he had won the spearfishing competition until the night that trophy was awarded.

George Ames, Raconteur Extraordinaire: Tall, lean, white-haired, soft-spoken and easy-going, George was one of the most popular and best-loved members of the club. He was given the

Bullshit Award not for a single incident, but rather for the entire body of his works. He was an exceptionally fine storyteller who could suck you in every time, even though you knew better than to believe a word he said. Additionally, he frequently brought along on the dive trips his 10-year-old daughter, who was a world-class poker player, fleecing everyone who attempted to challenge her.

Dennis Wodjan, Official Club Pollack: Dennis always had a twinkle in his eyes and a knowing grin on his face, even when we subjected him to good-natured ribbing about his Polish heritage, complete with all those tasteless Polish jokes. But he did get his revenge, and it was sweet. At the time of this incident, attempts were being made to farm Maine lobsters here in California waters since they are generally considered more tasty and succulent than our local spiny ones. These attempts were largely unsuccessful. On one of our dive trips, unobserved by anyone on the boat, Dennis smuggled on board a live Maine lobster that he had purchased at a local market. Also unobserved, he took the creature with him on his first dive. When he returned to the boat, he climbed on board shouting excitedly and waving his prize triumphantly. Everyone on board was instantly stricken with a severe case of Bug Fever of the Maine variety and gathered around Dennis as he described where he had found his prey. The location, of course, was a reef far away from the boat and down-current, but that did not deter the hoards of eager divers who quickly suited up and raced to be the first to reach the hunting grounds. Dennis just stood on deck with that twinkle in his eye and that knowing grin on his face.

Lynn Eldridge, wife of Dirty Jack: By the official rules of the competition, the founders of the trophy were ineligible for the award and a single individual could win the award only once, after which they became members of the award selection committee. Although Dirty Jack himself was ineligible for the Bullshit Award, since he was one of its founders and a member of the selection committee, his friends, spouse, and other companions were of course fair game. One year, Jack's wife, Lynn, became the target. And just what was it that she did to deserve such a fate? Well, she and Jack planned and executed a party to which they invited all of their friends. Ostensibly, the occasion was just a party. But as the evening's festivities warmed up, Jack and Lynn suddenly suggested some impromptu entertainment: a slave auction—just for fun of course.

Now understand that Lynn is a very liberated and independent woman, a research scientist with a Ph.D., who makes it very clear that self-determination is the only option. But this same Lynn now volunteered to get the action started by being the first slave to be auctioned.

Jack acted as auctioneer, but that didn't stop him from bidding, and—surprise, surprise—he ended up as the high bidder. All of us in attendance, particularly the women, were by this time completely dumbfounded, wondering if all that nitrogen from all those dives had finally rotted Lynn's brain or if perhaps the stress of Jack's career as an attorney had finally caused him to go over the edge.

Well, the mystery was solved soon enough when Jack and Lynn announced that the purpose of the party, the reality behind the slave auction smoke screen, was their wedding. At this point they called the minister forward and proceeded to go through a complete and genuine marriage ceremony. Clearly, Lynn was justly deserving of the David-Daniels Bullshit Award, and what made it especially delicious was that the awards committee met without Jack to make the decision, allowing Jack to believe that someone else was getting the award. He did not know that his wife was the recipient until he pulled the tape off the engraved plaque at the awards banquet. Ah, the look on his face was wonderful to behold as he realized that he had been bamboozled by his own selection committee!

Tom Kelly, Official Club Leprechaun: Sometimes, efforts to win the Bullshit Award backfired. Tom conspired with his wife Molly by allowing her to claim that she had captured one of Tom's lobsters, which put her in the lead for the Women's Lobster Trophy. Tom thought for sure that Molly would win the Bullshit Award for this one, but instead it was awarded to Tom himself. To this day, the general suspicion is that in fact the award was not for this specific incident but rather for the entire body of Tom's works. Being full-blooded Irish, redheaded, ornery on general principle, and mischievous in the extreme, Tom's storytelling skills are exceptional, as is his ability to mimic practically any foreign accent. To top it all off, he can improvise quirky little ditties on the fly, which he sings merrily, sounding for all the world like the Great Leprechaun himself.

✳   ✳   ✳

Besides these illustrious winners of the Bullshit Award, there are many club members whom I remember with great fondness:

There is Bonnie Cardone, who joined the club just a few months before I did. Each of us looked up to the other, assuming that the other was an experienced diver, not realizing until many years later that we had both been certified at almost the same time. In 1977, Bonnie became the first woman president of the club since the year of its inception, 1959, when Liz Johns was named first president. Bonnie, however, decided that being president was not sufficient, so she crowned herself Queen and ruled imperiously. Although her reign lasted only a year, to this day she is still known as Queen Bonnie. She and I founded the 10 O'clock Club, a very exclusive sub-group of the Fins, which has one cardinal rule: never dive before 10 o'clock in the morning. Unless of course there are mitigating circumstances, such as a flat, sunny morning at Wilson's Rock. Bonnie and I were also honored to have a reef named after us in the Sea of Cortez: Bonnith and Judith Rocks off Isla San Diego. The Skipper of the Marisla had at first suggested Judy and Bonnie Rocks, but Queen Bonnie insisted on top billing, so I insisted on top spelling.

And Paul Doose: Paul was another of the soft-spoken ones— tall, lanky and handsome, always busy gathering goodies on the dives to take back to his students. He frequently brought little handcrafted items, made from bits of shell or driftwood, to our meetings and was full of information about the islands and the living things that inhabited the oceans. And thanks to him, most everyone in the club had the opportunity to become a Grunion Mamma. Every year, Paul would go out and gather up a good supply of grunion eggs when those marvelous little fish made their orgiastic mating runs on the local beaches. He would keep the eggs packed in sand, and properly moist with seawater for the prescribed period of time, and then bring them to one of the club meetings. After his talk, which described the fish and their mating habits, he would provide everyone with paper cups, each containing a small scoop of the sand and egg mixture. By adding sea-water and stirring with a swizzle stick, we could simulate the effect of high tide on the eggs and the tiny grunion would hatch before our very eyes, popping from their little eggs and swimming frantically round and round in our paper cups.

And I can't forget Jerry "Sheets" Martin, one of those quiet, unassuming guys who appeared to be perfectly normal, as befitting someone who worked for IBM. But when you got to know him, he would reveal his true personality, which was just a tad bit off kilter, slightly bent and delightfully quirky. He would show up on the dive boats with the lunch that his wife had packed for him, and while the rest of us had to be content with hamburgers on paper plates, Jerry would dine by candlelight on crab mousse accompanied with wine in a real wine glass, wiping his mouth stylishly with his linen napkin. On occasion he would offer to share his bunk with one of the women divers on board, telling them that he had brought with him real sheets so they wouldn't have to use the rough wool blankets provided by the boat. Hence, of course, his nickname. But don't let the linens and crab mousse fool you – Jerry was a damn good diver too. He once bagged a 20-pound halibut by stabbing it with his knife, holding on to the knife handle with one hand and the protruding knife-blade with the other hand as he swam back to the boat. He had to do it that way since he had taken neither spear nor fish stringer with him on the dive.

And Connie Weiss: Connie is one of those "Earth Mother" types, soft and mellow and spiritual, a yoga teacher by trade. I've always felt a special bond with her, knowing that we share a similar love for the ocean and the life within it. We have spent many long moments sitting together on the deck of a boat, quietly listening and observing and being. But one of my most vivid memories of Connie is from the evening of the annual club luau in 1984. At the time, the trophy competition for lobsters was divided by gender, with one trophy for the men and another for the women. Invariably, as much as we women hated to acknowledge it, the men's trophy winner was a larger lobster than was the women's. In 1984, however, for the first time in the history of the competition, the women's trophy winner was larger than the men's—and it was Connie who had won. When the award was announced, she performed a remarkably gleeful and animated victory dance all the way up to the podium and all the way back to her seat. And, she spent the rest of the evening gloating and grinning, exuberantly victorious. Thereafter, the two trophies were combined into a single award, regardless of gender.

But for the all-time winner of the Club's Fabulous Fish stories, I have to nominate Dirty Jack himself, for an incident that occurred on a rare, calm day at Wilson's Rock in August of 1978. All of us were excited by the excellent diving conditions in such a beautiful spot and we eagerly suited up. And then we saw them: Three small, blue sharks swimming very near the boat. We saw two more glide past as we headed for the gate to jump in the water. For all his years as a diver, and for all of his energy and enthusiasm and bravado, Dirty Jack hates and fears sharks. At the mere thought of these creatures, he turns white. He refuses even to consider entering the water.

However, the skipper reassured us that these particular sharks were merely babies, and besides, blues are not at all aggressive. So we all jumped. On that first dive, my husband and I saw three more sharks, one of them close to five feet long, but none of them gave any signs of being interested in us so we continued our dive as usual.

We were resting between dives on the aft deck when Dirty Jack and Lynn returned from their dive. Jack was white as a sheet and very animated: "There was a shark following us! A big blue!" Spluttering as he doffed his gear, he held up three fingers. "Three times! That damned shark bumped me three times!! It was trying to get our fish!"

Both Jack and Lynn had speared fish, which they were bringing back with them. After the shark bumped Jack for the third time, he grabbed Lynn's fish stringer and released it, hoping that the shark would then leave them alone. "I was in fear for my life," he exclaimed, several times. As Jack told his story, Lynn stood on the deck nearby, looking nonplussed but not saying a word. Someone asked Jack why he had kept his own fish, while letting Lynn's fish go. "Because hers was bleeding," he shot back. Lynn's mouth dropped open and a look of utter incredulity took over her face as she stared at the large fish dangling from Jack's weight belt. It was dripping blood—lots of it—all over the deck.

But justice ultimately prevailed. On the very next dive, Lynn found her fish, still on its stringer with not so much as a nibble of flesh missing from it, and she brought it back to the boat triumphantly. It wasn't bleeding.

Trust

Fat little seal pup
Asking with your big brown eyes
For a belly-rub.

Idyll

I stepped quietly out of the cabin onto the aft deck. The morning had dawned fresh and clear, giving every sign that it was going to be yet another perfect day in paradise. It was Sunday, the last day of our 4-day Thanksgiving weekend, and we were anchored off the northwest side of Santa Barbara Island, 40 miles from the California mainland. After a smooth transit from Long Beach Harbor, we had celebrated Thanksgiving with friends and acquaintances on other boats anchored in Cat Harbor, the far side of the isthmus near the west end of Catalina. But Catalina gets pretty crowded on holiday weekends, even under water on the reefs. We were anxious to get away from it all and the weather had been so calm and warm and clear that we decided the next day to head for Santa Barbara, another 20 miles or so west of Catalina.

I stood silently, breathing in the sharp smell of salt water and kelp, listening to the perpetual *oaark-oaark-oaark* of the hundreds of sea lions in the rookery just west of our anchorage. The surface of the water was smooth and glossy like a vast sea of liquid mercury. It lapped gently against the 30-foot-long sides of the *C-Roam-Ance*, moving the deck under my bare feet ever so slightly. I kept my knees flexed and my stance wide to compensate and focused on the view before me as the breeze ruffled through my hair. It was past sunrise and the morning sea was brilliant out beyond the shadow cast by the 300-foot hills of the tiny island. I closed my eyes and let the fierce intensity of its fire wash over my face and burn off the slight chill on my body that was left over from the darkness. My husband and our three companions were still asleep in the cabin. I cherished moments like these when I could drift alone with my thoughts in the freshness of the early morning, taking in and savoring the sights and sounds and smells of the sea and sky and island.

The soft, gently rolling hills of the island were glowing now in that rich, radiant shade of gold that the native dried grasses take on under a low November sun. Our rainy season would not start for probably another month, so it would be at least two more months before the island assumed its mossy green winter coat. Clumps of low, dark green shrubs accented the hillsides here and there, but the island has no trees so the only thing that breaks the smooth, lyrical flow of its contours is the abrupt transition from golden hillside to the rugged, dark craggy cliffs which fall to the ocean several hundred feet below. The sea lions had established their rookery at the base of these cliffs, their bodies sprawled helter-skelter not only on the narrow sandy beaches but also up on the lower ramparts of the cliff face.

My eyes followed a dark, glistening adult female as she hip-hopped and slinked from the water's edge across the sand and then clambered up on a low ledge to rest and sun herself dry. As awkward and cumbersome as their bodies are on land, these creatures are remarkably fast and agile in the water. My mind wandered back to the previous day when we had watched in fascination as three young adults, each about seven feet long, frolicked and tussled near us while we poked around the edge of the reef. The animals rolled and tumbled, looped and chased, nipping playfully at each other and occasionally swooping past us, as if they were checking to make sure we were watching and enjoying the show they were staging.

The loud disapproving roar of a very large bull brought me back to the present. He sat majestically on an outcropping of rock near the base of the cliff, the front half of his massive body starkly upright, his snout pointed up toward the breaking sunlight as he raged and warned and boasted of his powers. I smiled my approval, stretched long and leisurely, and padded to the transom to check on the water's visibility in anticipation of the new day's diving adventures.

As I leaned over the railing I was startled to see a baby sea lion sound asleep on the swim-step, completely oblivious to my presence. No more than three feet long, it lay stretched out on the wooden grate, its fur light gray and fluffed, a sign that it had been out of the water for several hours. I could discern a pair of tiny external ears held close against a well-molded little head. The head gathered into a puppy-like snout that ended in a wet black nose, accented with a fine set of whiskers. The curve of its head dipped slightly but seamlessly into the fat round torso, tapering gently to its dark leathery rear flippers. Its left front flipper was stretched out toward the water, but its right flipper was not visible. It was tucked under its body.

Entranced, I stood and watched the little creature as it lay sleeping. I scarcely dared to breathe for fear of waking it and frightening it away. After what seemed like an eternity, but was probably only 15 or 20 minutes, the cabin door opened behind me and Dick, one of our diving companions, stepped out on deck. I quickly signaled him to come over quietly and look at our visitor. The surprise on his face spread into a broad grin of delight, and we went back into the cabin so I could tell him how I had discovered the animal.

Soon our other shipmates were up: my husband Jon, our friend Paul, who was the owner and skipper of the *C-Roam-Ance*, and his girlfriend Jackie. We cautioned each in turn so they could go outside and get a good look without disturbing the little tyke's slumber. Of course, we couldn't maintain such control and silence for long and soon our delight bubbled into enough commotion that we awakened our visitor.

I was leaning over the transom and looking at him when he jolted awake. His huge, perfectly round black eyes suddenly wide open, he lifted his head and looked at me. He flinched, as though starting to slip into the water, but he didn't bolt. I held his gaze and smiled at him warmly. He returned my gaze and stayed. I spoke to him softly and gently, to welcome him aboard and invite him to stay and visit. He looked at me quizzically, trying to puzzle out the meaning of these strange sounds. After some time, he relaxed, laid his head back down, and gave a contented sigh.

Emboldened by his show of acceptance and trust, I slowly and carefully walked to the far side of the transom and climbed over to stand on the swim-step. Once more, the little guy raised his head and watched. I continued to speak quietly to him as I moved slowly closer and closer, hunching down to appear as small as possible and as close to his eye level as I could. I reached out and gently touched his forehead. He blinked and lifted his head up to meet my hand. Within a half-hour, I was stroking his head and scratching him under his chin as though we were best friends.

From here on, the five of us took turns visiting with our new shipmate as we prepared and ate our breakfast and began getting our diving gear together for the day. For a while, we worried about whether our friend was sick. But he looked quite sleek and fat and healthy, with rich full fur and bright shiny alert eyes. He didn't act weak, merely contented and relaxed. So we stopped fussing. Paul and Dick suited up and jumped into the water, using the mid-ship portside gate to minimize the chance of disturbing the baby, who was still lazing about on the starboard side of the swim-step.

I decided not to go diving this day, but I put on my swimsuit and got into the water at the stern, to gather some kelp. I brought a few strands of the large, leathery-gold giant kelp back to the boat and offered bits of it to our little friend. He wasn't wild about the leaf-like blades, but munched away happily on the little football-shaped float-bulbs that form at the base of each blade. In the meantime, Jon cleaned a couple of abalone that we had found the day before and we offered the tough meaty trimmings to our friend. These were also a big hit.

Suddenly, the little guy heaved himself off the swim-step and splashed into the water. My heart sank—he was leaving us! He turned and swam along the starboard side of the boat, rounded the bow, swam the length of the port side, and flopped back up onto the swim-step in his old spot! I greeted him joyfully with an offering of crunchy kelp-bulbs.

Occasionally throughout the morning, he would once more heave himself off the swim-step and do a turn or two around the boat before reclaiming his berth. Every time he left I feared the worst, but every time he came back. He seemed completely unconcerned by our activities as we went about shuffling gear, diving, cleaning game, and talking and joking among ourselves. Several times I jumped off the side of the boat and swam around it, as our friend had done. I splashed out into the thick kelp bed, alternately floating and kelp-crawling, looking for treasures such as kelp snails. I found several, and delighted in watching as their black-spotted, pumpkin-yellow bodies glided along the kelp strands, carrying with them their smoothly curved rusty colored shells. I plucked a few more small clumps of kelp to feed our visitor: I hoped that I was picking the most tender and tasty morsels for him. Regardless, he seemed to enjoy them.

Inevitably, as much as I wished that I had the power to stop it, the sun continued its upward climb. When it reached its apex, we began putting away our gear and tidying things up in preparation for our homeward journey. Our little visitor was still lazing about on the swim-step when Paul started up the engine. Startled by the loud sputter and rumble, he quickly dived into the water and disappeared under the canopy of the kelp. I can't be certain, but I think that was his head I saw pop up on the far side of the kelp as we motored away. I stood and watched until the bobbing dark head receded into a tiny black spot in the distance. Then, it disappeared from sight.

As the engine droned on, the island slipped farther and farther away. Once more, I must return to the "real world" and leave behind this alternate universe. I miss my little friend and, across the years, I have continued to cherish the memories of the time we spent together. Every time I return to Santa Barbara Island, I watch eagerly for the sea lions, wondering whether he is still among them, whether the little ones I see now are his offspring. Wondering if he ever dreams of that warm November day long ago that he shared with those strange beings from far away.

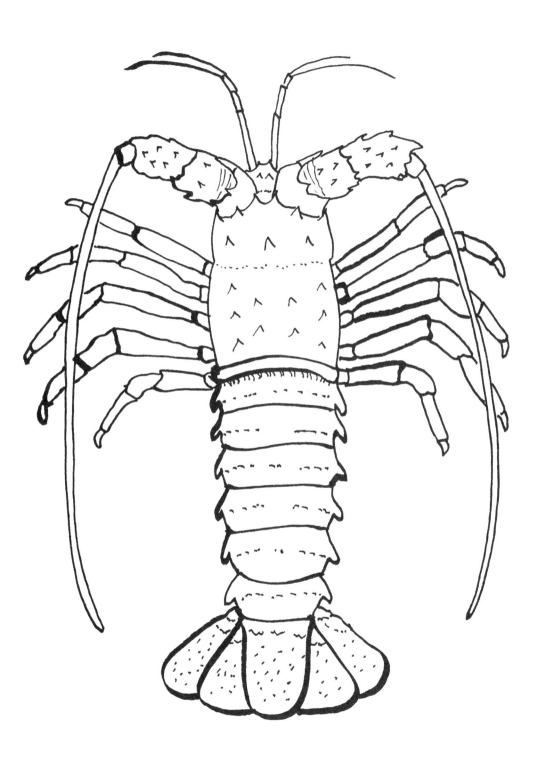

The Thrill of the Hunt

The lobster sat motionless, its beady little eyes staring at me smugly, its long stiff antennae waving slowly, as though daring me to make my move. I'd never thought of myself as a hunter, but this was the first time I'd ever seen a lobster face-to-face, outside of a restaurant holding tank, and I was instantly seized by a severe case of "Bug Fever." My heart raced and my mouth watered at the thought of succulent white lobster meat dipped into freshly melted butter.

I sized up the situation, noting the arrangement of rocks around the beast's lair, planning how I would lunge to grab the base of its antennae. I knew my strike would have to be quick and sure or the crafty creature would retreat as swiftly as a lightening bolt back into the depths of its cave. The bubbles from my heavy breathing boiled furiously around my head as I made my move. My swift and deadly lunge met only fluid, empty ocean. "Damn!" I scolded myself. "I've got to be quicker than that!"

Three more times I found fresh prey and repeated the same futile ritual. By this time the "fever" was raging, my blood coursing hot and feral through my veins. I had to succeed: I had to catch, I had to kill. I looked around and saw Jon going after yet another bug. I sent a fierce thought-wave toward him, willing him to succeed, and then I noticed that he had laid his spear down nearby.

I was desperate. I grabbed the long yellow fiberglass pole and spun around full-circle, looking for something—anything—that I could shoot. I'd never used a pole-spear before, but I had watched Jon use it. All I had to do was loop the rubber tubing over my hand, stretch it forward as far as I could along the shaft, aim it at a fish, and release.

A 2-foot long Sheephead mosied toward me, its large black head crowned by a prominent bump, the mark of a mature male.

I had to hold the spear with both hands to keep it properly cocked as I waited for the fish to come near. As soon as it was within range, I released my grip and the pole shot forward, directly toward the side of the fish. It bounced off. A wave of exasperation swept over me as I realized that I didn't have enough strength to shoot the spear effectively.

Without wavering, the fish continued to swim slowly past me, either completely oblivious to the threat of my presence or confident that I wasn't a threat. I cocked the spear once more and released it. Again it bounced off. My frustration was climbing ever higher. But wait—the fish shuddered several times, tilted on its side, and sank motionless to the bottom. Apparently, it was more stunned than I was and it remained that way long enough for me to pick it up by the gills and secure it on Jon's fish stringer. I was elated: I had achieved "first blood," even though my victim not only wasn't bleeding, but didn't have a mark on him.

Somehow, though, a large, and remarkably stupid, fish was not a satisfying substitute for a tasty lobster, so we continued our hunt. Finally, as our air supply was running low, we spotted a sizeable bug sitting in a very accessible hole. I swooped and was able to grab the bug by the body, but I couldn't pull it out. It had its legs firmly wrapped around a big rock embedded in the sand. Impasse.

Jon circled around the back, motioned to me that he had found a backdoor entrance to the hole, and then disappeared behind the rock. Very shortly, I could feel his hand tugging on the tail of the bug. We tugged and wrestled mightily, stirring up the sandy bottom into an ever-expanding cloud. Suddenly, the lobster released its grip on the rock and I was able to pull it out. As I backed away from the hole, a hand materialized before my mask dangling a large lobster tail. Startled, I looked at the now-tail-less lobster in my hands. We had managed not only to separate the lobster from its rock, but had also separated its head and body from its tail!

That evening we dined on fresh lobster while our cats devoured huge servings of fresh Sheephead. In the years since then I have become a somewhat more skilled hunter and we have enjoyed many feasts of fresh seafood, but we have also found other ways of hunting that are equally satisfying. For many years, I kept a saltwater aquarium, not for tropical fish purchased in a store, but for local creatures, brought back from our dives. Armed only with a lidded Tupperware tub, I stalked and collected snails, anemones, small rocks covered with various seaweeds, nudibranchs, and other slow-moving life-forms to put in my tank. Nudibranchs are small sea slugs, which resemble our common garden slugs like a circus clown resembles a monk.

I learned the hard way about the food chain in the ocean. On one dive, I had found three or four different species of splendidly colored nudibranchs, which I was carrying in my Tupperware tub. Then I added a new creature I had never seen before—a large, navy-blue slug with yellow racing stripes. By the time I got back to the boat and opened the tub, all that remained in it was the new creature. The reference book I consulted identified the creature as a Navanax, a carnivorous sea slug that specializes in eating nudibranchs.

The day after I had added a Kellet's Whelk snail to the tank, I discovered that they too are carnivorous; overnight it had killed and eaten my prize Queen Tegula snail. Another time, I found a beautiful little striped shore crab in a tide pool and everyday when I came home from work, there was one less living mussel in my small mussel colony in the corner of the tank.

To add more variety to the tank, I purchased a slurp-gun. This is a fiberglass tube about two feet long that is constructed like a gigantic syringe without a needle. By starting with the plunger fully in and rapidly pulling it back, suction is created and water rushes into the tube, slurping in with it any unwary creatures nearby. With this weapon I was able to capture small fish including a 4-inch white Black-eyed Goby and several tiny Blue-banded Gobies, which are fire-orange in color with 5–6 neon-blue vertical stripes.

One day, I stumbled upon a Mermaid's Purse. This is a golden, leathery, oblong container about six inches long with curling tendrils extending from all four corners. I was very excited by this find because I knew that it is actually the egg case for a Swell Shark. I kept the Purse in my tank, watching it daily. By holding it in front of a flashlight, I could see the shadowy yolk and embryo within. As the weeks went by, the embryo grew and took shape, curling around its shrinking yolk. Finally, one day when I came home from work, there was a tiny and perfectly formed Swell Shark swimming in the tank.

I named him Spot and fed him raw fish out of my hand. He grew to about 6 inches in length and did quite well in the tank until summer arrived and the tank water began to get too warm. There were no chillers available for aquariums, only heaters for tropical fish. Jon built a cooling system, using an underwater pump sitting in a Styrofoam cooler, to pump ice water through coiled plastic tubing submerged in the tank. This helped a lot but in the heat of the summer it required two 25-pound blocks of ice a day, one in the morning and one in the evening, to keep the tank water cold enough. August arrived and with it a fierce heat wave. Even two blocks of ice a day was not enough: The water temperature rose into the high 70s and Spot died. We buried him in my rose garden and I shut the aquarium down. These days I do most of my hunting with an underwater camera, collecting slides to share with my family and friends, to show them the wonderful creatures and beautiful reefs that I love so much.

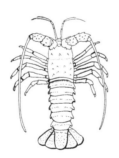

Lost

Engulfed in dark depths—
How can I find my way back?
By looking within.

Boomerang!

The anchor chain leaped and clattered furiously as it plunged headlong into the cold, ink-colored sea. Moments later the sound shifted abruptly from the clanking of chain to the swift shushing of the 2-inch anchor line as it followed the chain into the deep. Foot after foot of line rushed madly over the transom while the crew watched from a respectful distance, ready to leap into action if anything went wrong. Finally, the movement slowed and the crew and skipper went about the careful business of ensuring that the anchor was set properly.

It was early morning on the second day of our dive trip. The sky was overcast, giving a pre-dawn darkness to the scene, even though it was past 8 a.m. We had finished our breakfast and I was sipping my second cup of tea as I sized up the situation. We were anchoring at an underwater pinnacle named Boomerang, miles from nowhere, in the depths between the northern Channel Islands and the mainland of Southern California. The exact location of the pinnacle was privileged information, known to the skipper of the *Truth* and to very few others. Like many such locations, it was unprotected by any nearby land masses and usually the surface conditions were too rough to permit diving. But today was an exception. Barely.

I sized up the swells as they rolled under the boat: about five to six feet from trough to peak. Add a bit of chop to that and it was clear the decision to dive or not had to be made carefully. I learned long ago as a novice diver never to argue with the ocean. She was much, much bigger than I was and would have her way, regardless. All that we mere mortals could do was learn how to read her moods and work within her constraints. To try anything more was to move beyond reasonable risk toward potential disaster—indeed, even death.

I thought back over the diving of the previous day: It had been a good day for me. The diving conditions had been easy and we had taken our time, with no attempt to push hard or perform macho heroics. And then that day, over three years ago, flashed clearly into my mind. I remembered collapsing exhausted onto the living room couch, too fatigued even to cry, unable to move for the rest of the day and evening. The reason: I had walked three blocks to the mailbox and back home, the first time I had ventured any distance from the house on my own in over five months.

In spite of my exhaustion, however, that simple walk had been the beginning of my recovery. I began to improve gradually: There were many ups and downs, but the overall trend was slowly up. Over the course of three years I had finally reached the point where I felt strong enough to try diving again. I had been out of the water for almost four years, but now I was on a boat and I had made two dives. Granted they were easy dives, not nearly up to my old standards, but it was a start.

I looked up from my empty teacup as my reverie brought me back to the present. Then I noticed something very unusual: the crew had rigged a line from the anchor line back along the side of the boat to the swim-step at the stern. I frowned at the mystery, looked forward again at the anchor line, and then I understood. A frothy white V-shaped wake was clearly visible where the anchor line entered the water and the line itself shuddered and hummed from the tension. There was a wicked current running!

My husband joined me on deck as the skipper made his pre-dive announcement. There would be time for only one jump here, due to the conditions. The anchor was on the pinnacle, the top of which was about 80 feet deep. The current was running strong and the skipper advised using the extra rope to pull ourselves from the side of the boat forward to the anchor line, then follow it down to the pinnacle. Jon and I discussed the situation; should we go or not? He said he was not comfortable with the conditions and did not want to dive. That gave me pause, knowing the strength of his 6-foot-4-inch body and his love of diving, especially pinnacle diving. We have always had an agreement never to push the other person into diving if they had the least hesitation. It was too dangerous for such non-sense. So I respected his decision but I was disappointed; we had never before had the opportunity to dive Boomerang and it was said to be very beautiful.

I looked at the gray sky, the rolling swells, the chop, and the wake of the anchor line. I knew that I had to do it. It was rare. It was beautiful.

I had to know. Was I once more strong and healthy or still in the grip of my illness? It was called Chronic Fatigue Immune Deficiency Syndrome or CFIDS. The name sounded harmless enough, but it was more—much more—than fatigue. It was an overwhelming, all-consuming lassitude through every fiber of my being. It was mental fogginess and confusion so severe that my vocabulary was reduced to a few hundred words, which I frequently could not compose into coherent sentences. It was constant pain, in muscles and joints, that felt like arthritis and charley horses and massive bruises. It was eruptions of red-hot itching welts the size of dinner plates. It was constant dizziness that made me hug the walls as I walked, for fear of falling. It was endless nausea, and finally, it was depression that grew and grew until I began thinking that it would be better to die than to live if there was no end to this disease. But on this day, it seemed that it had ended and I felt a compulsion to test myself, to see where my limits were now.

I noticed that our friend Andre was donning his wetsuit, but his wife was not. He agreed to be my dive buddy. We discussed our plan; we would follow the skipper's advice and then stay within the top 20 feet or so of the pinnacle. Jon helped me with my gear and gently fussed a little. "Be careful, don't do anything stupid, come back safe, I love you."

Using the bow entry would put us very close to the anchor line, minimizing the distance and time we would have to spend on the rough surface in the current. I jumped first, my stomach doing its usual half-somersault as I plunged 10 feet into the water. I didn't feel the cold water as it seeped into my wetsuit; I was too intent on reaching the current line. I could feel the water tugging at my gear as I pulled myself forward and grabbed the anchor line. The force of the current held me horizontal as I waited for Andre; I felt like a flag flapping in the wind. Andre arrived and we hauled ourselves hand over hand down the rope. I was breathing hard and heavy from the effort, but my arms felt strong and I kept my face pointed down and into the current to keep the water from ripping my mask off.

The current did not diminish as we descended. It was still as strong at 60 feet as it had been on the surface. My focus was sharp and narrow; the only things that existed in my universe besides Andre and I were the dark current and that rope.

We reached the end of the rope and continued down the chain. It was very dark at this depth, but the water was clear and we could now see the pinnacle in the distance. The anchor chain dipped down about 10 feet below the top of the pinnacle and then rose up, draping over the crest, a perfect anchorage. We continued our slow and laborious hand-over-hand journey until we reached the crest and moved down the opposite side.

Suddenly, the world was calm and tranquil. Here the current could not touch us and we looked at each other in surprise. The delight dancing in Andre's eyes reflected my own feelings. We paused briefly to check our respective air and depth gauges, and the time remaining as indicated by our dive computers. I had used about a third of my air in that laborious descent, but now my breathing slowed to its normal rhythm. We were at 87 feet, with 26 minutes remaining at that depth. We pantomimed to each other, agreeing to descend a little further and work our way back and forth, and gradually up, the narrow face of the pinnacle.

We turned our attention to the huge rock form before us and an explosion of life greeted our eyes. Every square inch of rock was covered with sea life. There were masses of great black mussels as wide as my hand and several inches longer; hundreds of tiny strawberry anemones, each clonal colony a different shade of pink or orange or lavender; red-orange tealia anemones with their white polka-dotted stems; lacy white metridiums like giant powderpuffs on gracefully swaying foot-long stalks. Nestled in between were patches of encrusting sponges, leafy clumps of brown and green and red algae, and the conical forms of large barnacles, their long slender gills grasping rhythmically and delicately for microscopic nutrients in the cold rich water.

We took our time, nosing leisurely among the rocks, looking for the smaller gems: the smooth oval brown and white shells of the chestnut cowry, partially covered by the snail's tan mantle with its black polka dots; the twin multi-colored whirls of feather-duster worms; and—most prized of all—the riotous colors and forms of that impossible creature, the nudibranch. I watched a Spanish Shawl nudibranch as it "danced" in the water just inches off the rock, its tiny, intensely purple slug-like body undulating back and forth, its bright-orange fringe of cerata rippling and swaying. Andre motioned me over to see a white dorid nudibranch, flat and oval with four large dark-brown rings on its back, carrying its gills like a tiny tree just behind the rings.

All too soon we realized that we had worked our way back up, almost to the top of the pinnacle and our gauges indicated it was time to end the dive. Andre pointed to the anchor and motioned that we should start up the chain.

As soon as we topped the pinnacle, the fierce current caught us and tried to drag us away. I grabbed hold of the anchor chain and narrowed my focus once more to concentrate on my grip. I felt a momentary panic as I thought about the 80 feet of water above me and the long, slow ascent I had to make. But my determination overruled the fear. I breathed deeply and began my hand-over-hand climb. Up and up I climbed along the chain, each link marking my progress. The pinnacle disappeared from sight and I was completely surrounded by the featureless dark blue depths.

Once I passed the transition from chain to rope, the only way to tell that I was moving upward in that vast cold darkness was to watch my bubbles as I exhaled. I was breathing heavily again and I tensed, fighting the urge to scramble up the line to the surface that I knew waited so far above. I concentrated on my bubbles, willing myself to ascend no faster than they did. Time ceased and I heard only the sound of my labored breathing and my body fighting the current.

Slowly, the blue around me lightened and shafts of yellow sun sparkled and danced around me. I let some air out of my vest to slow my ascent and then I was on the surface, with the bow of the boat plunging and leaping a few feet in front of me. I knew I had to keep my distance from the huge monster or it would crash down on top of me. I transferred rapidly to the current line, alternately tightening and relaxing my grip to control my movement as the current pushed me along the side of the boat. Within seconds, I was at the stern. I lunged at the swim-step as the current swept me past it and hauled myself onto its shuddering surface like a beached whale.

I laid on my stomach on the swim-step, too tired to stand up, riding out several violent rounds of up-and-down splashing and crashing before I was able to maneuver my finned feet under me and crawl up to the more stable wooden step at the base of the ladder. The waiting crewman removed my fins and gave the bottom of my tank a push to get me started up the ladder.

On deck, Jon waited anxiously. "How was it?" He asked, his blue eyes searching my face intently for any signs of distress. I clumsily pulled my mask off, my hands stiff and uncoordinated from the cold and the effort, and I beamed up at him.

"It was gorgeous," I answered. "I did it! I'm back."

I'd ask my friends to come and see
An octopus's garden with me.
I'd like to be under the sea
In an octopus's garden with you.
     — Richard Starkey

Octopus's Garden

THE GARDEN IN THE SAND

$\mathcal{I}$was pleased with my new mask. In addition to the usual front faceplate, it had clear glass side plates, which enabled me to use my peripheral vision instead of having to turn my head back and forth constantly to see from side to side. As I looked straight ahead I could see Jon off to my left about 10 feet away, kicking slowly and rhythmically on a course parallel to mine. We were doing something unusual today—exploring the sand flats, a change of pace from our usual diet of rocky reefs.

Like the land, the ocean has its deserts—vast expanses of sand that appear to the casual observer to be devoid of life. There are no winds here to create large rolling sand dunes, but the currents and constant surging action of the water create beautiful patterns of ripples across the surface of the sand. Without such ripples it would be impossible to tell if we were moving forward or backward—or sideways. The surge was strong enough today to move the top dusting of sand back and forth about six inches each way, creating an endless moving cloud of tiny grains. The water was clear and we were less than 30 feet deep so the sunlight penetrated well, dancing in animated ribbons of gold across the pale yellow sand. The shimmering sunlight, combined with the back-and-forth movement of the sand clouds and the nearly featureless bottom, made my head spin as my eyes sought in vain for something solid and defined and stationary to focus on. After a few minutes, realizing the futility of the effort, I chose to relax into the motion and enjoy the disorientation.

Up ahead, we could see a change in the landscape: dozens of—something—sticking up out of the sand. As we got closer I began to think we were swimming across the top of a very large desk punctuated with old-fashioned quill pens. Waving gently and gracefully, the sea pens expanded and contracted, furled and unfurled, as they fed on the tiny bits of food carried on the currents. Sea pens are colonial animals, closely related to corals. Although usually when we think of corals we envision large reef structures, there are many animals such as the sea pens that have adapted to life in the sand. One of my favorites is a close cousin of the sea pens, the sea pansy, which consists of a purple heart-shaped leathery structure called a rachis growing on a stalk. Sprinkled about on this purple rachis are small white flowery-looking animals, giving the overall structure the look of a floating purple garden of white flowers.

As we continued across the sand, we also found occasional tube anemones, their leathery tubes rooted deeply in the sand, housing a beautiful rosette-shaped anemone with long "petals" (actually stinging tentacles) that swayed gracefully in the current. We scanned the surface of the sand closely and sharply, looking for the tell-tale raised tracks of sand that would indicate the movements of the purple dwarf olives. These sand-dwelling snails live in beautiful shiny little white shells tinged with lavender and accents of dark gray. Usually the only way to see them is to find one of their trails, follow it to its end, and dig a few inches down into the sand, hoping of course that you had chosen the leading end of the trail.

We found no olives on this particular dive, but we did find another sand traveler: a 2-inch long shell encrusted with tiny fuzzy growths. The fact that its movement was not smooth and gliding, but rather jerky and irregular like a drunkard on a Saturday night binge, told us that the inhabitant was not a snail but a hermit crab. Jon picked it up and turned it over, and we caught a glimpse of the crab as it quickly withdrew back into the spirals of the shell leaving only its hairy, polka-dotted front legs and pincers revealed. Putting it down gently, we continued on our way.

Off in the distance ahead, Jon noticed something dark protruding from the bottom and we finned over toward it. When we got close enough, we realized that the "something" was a pair of foot-long dark brown pen shells, their pointed ends stuck down into the sand about a foot apart, their wide ends pointing up toward the surface and gaping open slightly as though they had been arranged that way deliberately. On closer inspection, we realized that one of the shells housed a small mottled brown octopus. The second shell was stuffed full of smaller empty shells of many different varieties, and the surrounding area was also a tidy pile of empty shells. What we had found was an octopus's house and its very neatly maintained garbage midden. We tried to coax the octopus out of his shell, but like most octopuses he was extremely shy and stayed curled up in the cozy protection of his lair.

IN THIS CASE IT REALLY IS GREEK

Since that first encounter in the sandy garden, I've had a number of other encounters with octopuses and, through reading and TV/video programs, I've learned that these are intelligent and fascinating creatures. The word octopus is derived from the Greek roots 'octo-', meaning eight, and 'pous-' meaning foot. Because the word is Greek, not Latin, the proper plural form is octopodes, not octopi, but the form 'octopuses' is also acceptable and is in fact more widely used. Octopuses are members of the class Cephalopoda, meaning head-foot, and are closely related to paper nautiluses, cuttlefish, squid, and the chambered nautiluses. The cephalopods have three hearts, blue blood, and a complex nervous system, including a multi-lobed brain. They swim using jet propulsion, create smoke screens by expelling ink, and change color, texture, and shape with amazing speed and skill.

Cephalopods may be very small or very large and can be found worldwide in habitats ranging from shallow sandy areas and tropical coral reefs to cold-water kelp beds and deep open water. Hollywood would have us believe that octopuses and squid are aggressive and hostile man-eaters, capable of capturing submarines and wreaking havoc on the Free World. This is not so. Generally, like our little friend in the pen shell, octopuses are shy and retiring, preferring to forage at night.

SURPRISINGLY SMART SUCKERS

Although they are mollusks, which means they are related to creatures such as oysters and abalone, the cephalopods are considered to be remarkably intelligent and recent research has shown clear indications of this intelligence. They learn rapidly to perform actions such as uncorking a glass container to get at the meal inside, even apparently learning merely by observing another ceph perform the trick in the tank next door. There are a number of reports of octopuses climbing out of their tank into a neighboring tank for a meal and then returning to their own tank. One researcher reports that his octopuses are sophisticated enough to play. Given an empty bottle, one creature repeatedly squirted it into the current so that the water circulation would push the bottle back, whereupon the octopus would squirt the bottle away again. This octopus played with the bottle non-stop for almost half an hour.

In addition to the capacity for play, the same researchers have found evidence of what they call "personality" variations, at least within one species of Pacific octopus. After observing 44 individuals over three years in a number of structured everyday situations, the researchers concluded that there were three discernable personality types: active, reactive, and avoiding. These types were illustrated by three particular individuals that had been given names by the aquarium staff: There was "Leisure Suit Larry," who was very active and exploratory; "Emily Dickinson," who usually hid behind some equipment at the back of the tank; and "Lucretia McEvil," who consistently rearranged and frequently dismantled anything that was put in the tank.

A segment of *Wild Discovery* (June, 2000) showed footage of a small red-and-white striped octopus that the researchers had named the "Wonderpus" for its remarkable behavior. It is capable of extending membranes along the length of its arms, spiraling the arms to form a webbed tent or umbrella over its prey. At another time, it curled its webbed arms up into pinwheel shapes, reminding me of a multi-armed circus muscleman flexing his biceps. The most remarkable footage of the segment, however, dealt with the Mimic octopus, found in the waters of Indonesia near Teluk Totok. Although most octopuses are capable of camouflage, using their shape-shifting and color-changing skills, the Mimic octopus takes this a few steps further, doing incredibly realistic impersonations of other creatures. By modifying its color pattern, skin texture, body shape and movements, the Mimic octopus becomes a sand anemone waving its tentacles in the currents, a flounder cruising the sandy bottom with its eyes protruding upward, a lionfish drifting lazily in the open water, a jellyfish pulsing near the surface, a carpet anemone withdrawing in on itself, a banded sea snake sniffing curiously around the rocks, or the head of a snake eel peering up out of a hole in the sand. Truly a tour-de-force performance!

GHOSTS ON THE YONGALA

But the most touching story that I have heard about octopuses is an experience related by Simon, a member of the crew of the *Paradise Sport* out of Papua New Guinea. Over the course of repeated dives on the *Yongala* wreck, Simon became friends with a pair of octopuses that lived there. They seemed to recognize him and would come out to greet and play with him whenever he appeared. On one dive, Simon left a fully-rigged tank with regulator on the wreck, planning to put it to use the next day. When he returned, he found the tank floating loose, emptied of its air. The regulator had not only been detached from the tank but had been dismantled, its hoses strewn about the wreck. No other divers had been on the wreck in the interim, so he was forced to conclude that the deed had been done by either the ghost of the *Yongala* or his two eight-legged friends.

Sadly, the two are no longer on the wreck. Octopuses have a very short lifespan, many species living only a year or two and mating only once. The pair on the *Yongala* mated and the male died shortly thereafter. The female holed up in the wreck and refused to come out, dying a short time after that. No young octopuses have been seen on the wreck.

So, if by chance some fine day you are finning through a sandy garden or rummaging through a crusty old wreck and you happen to stumble upon a tidy pile of empty shells or a completely disassembled regulator, be sure to take the time to stop and visit. You just may make a new friend and even learn a new trick or two.

Predator

The monster attacks,
Devouring everything—
Even its own young.

Here There Be Dragons

Obviously, it had seen us before we saw it. Vicki and I had been finning leisurely along the reef wall at about 65 feet, enjoying the clear tropical waters, the masses of corals, and schools of fish, completely oblivious to the dark and infinite blue depths to our left. Something—I'll never know what—made me stop and look outward.

From time immemorial, humans have explored and feared the ocean. Six hundred years ago, when the Earth was still flat, the maker of the Borgia map drew finned monsters the same size as the ships that floated on the map's choppy inked waves. A hundred years later, and a mere decade after Columbus returned from the New World, the maker of what may have been the first world globe engraved on its copper surface the words "Hic sunt dracones:" Here there be dragons.

A large dark form was hurtling directly toward us at an amazing speed. I knew instantly it was a shark—a very large shark. And I knew exactly what it was doing.

The attack posture of a shark is unmistakable. The beast arches its spine, head and tail downward, lifting its triangular dorsal fin upward like a banner being borne into battle. Its two pectoral fins are stiffened and angled down and out, acting as forward rudders or stabilizers. It swims by thrusting its lowered head and tail in unison, first to one side and then to the other. Were any other fish to try such a movement, it would look awkward and ridiculous. When a shark does it, it looks lethal.

For a split second, a fragment of a childhood nursery rhyme rang in my mind: "There was a crooked man and he walked a crooked mile …" But in the next split second, my body and my mind froze and I watched helplessly for an eternity as the beast hurtled toward me, its twisted crooked movements somehow sinuous and remarkably graceful. Three feet from my faceplate it lifted its head—ah, those teeth! Its white belly sweeping up and over us, it circled to our right and barreled back out into the blue. I was stunned. I turned to look at Vicki. I could hear her screaming through her regulator and her wild eyes filled her mask behind her faceplate.

Five years earlier, I had seen that same attack posture executed over and over again by my 6-inch long pet shark, Spot, every time I held a small piece of raw fish in the aquarium to feed him. He was a beautiful little Swell Shark, golden brown with mottled white markings and black spots. My friend Marie delighted in asking, "Hey, Judy, how's your pet shark doing?" whenever there were strangers present. We both loved to watch their faces when I told them that I fed Spot by hand. Having such an exotic pet and sharing the experience with others was a lot of fun.

This was no fun at all. As Vicki screamed, I nodded my head vigorously in agreement and pounded my chest with my fist to communicate how fiercely my heart was leaping. We backed up against the reef wall, side by side, and looked back out into the blue. The shark was turning now, just at the edge of our vision. To our horror, it once again assumed the attack posture and came charging toward us. It was about seven feet long, sleek and solid, its skin a bronze color on top, shading to a creamy color on its belly. The rear margins of its tail were dark.

The Bronze Whaler (*Carcharhinus brachyurus*) is a member of the family Carcharinidae, the Requiem sharks. Requiem is a Latin word meaning "to rest again" and is the first word in the Roman Catholic Mass for the dead. There are over 100 species of sharks in the Requiem family, including the Oceanic Whitetip, the Tiger, Bull, Lemon, Whitetip Reef, Blacktip Reef, Gray Whaler—and of course, the Bronze Whaler. According to the International Shark Attack File (ISAF), of the top 20 species responsible for attacks on humans, 15 are Requiems. The Bronze Whaler is 12th on the list, with 11 confirmed attacks, nine of those unprovoked.

As the Whaler charged toward us a second time, I thought about how large it was and how utterly defenseless we were. At seven feet long, it probably weighed close to 400 pounds. Neither Vicki nor I had anything even remotely resembling a weapon. I looked at the small yellow flashlight I held in my hand and I thought to myself, Well, they're supposed to have very tender noses. If he comes at me, I'll just punch him in the snout with this. *I looked back out at the Fate speeding toward us and then once more my mind and body froze.*

Over the three decades I have been diving, I have encountered various species of sharks countless times. The first shark I ever saw was a 6-foot Lemon shark in the Caribbean, on my honeymoon. I bought a shark-tooth pendant to commemorate the occasion and I wear it frequently as my good-luck charm. Besides my dear little pet Spot, I have shared the joys of the California kelp beds with sleek, graceful Blue sharks, sedentary Angel sharks and homely Horned sharks. In the Sea of Cortez, I have watched as schools of Scalloped Hammerheads cruised past, looking like patterned blue wallpaper. In the South Pacific I have enjoyed the company of dozens of Whitetip Reef sharks, some of which followed me around like puppy dogs. In addition to sharks, I have seen stingrays, electric rays, Moray eels, large schools of barracuda, and four of the highly poisonous black-banded sea snakes. I have never been attacked, though I was sometimes frightened.

Right now, I was terrified. This Whaler clearly meant business. Back arched, pectorals down, the beast charged again straight toward us. We huddled closer together, tight against the reef wall and watched numbly. I raised my arm and hand with the flashlight as a last simple, hopeless thought flickered through my consciousness: This is it. *And then once more, at the last moment, the Whaler pulled his snout up and swept up*

and over us, turning back out into the open ocean. My eyes followed piercingly, willing the beast to disappear. Smaller and darker and smaller it shrank, until it melted at last into the outer darkness.

The ISAF statistics include records for 882 attacks on humans that have been documented around the world since 1580. A National Audubon Society Report indicates that the commercial shark fishery in Florida caught 4.8 million pounds of sharks in one year (1996). According to Jonathan Bird, an award-winning underwater cinematographer: "An estimated 350 tons of shark fins (for shark fin soup) is consumed every year. This translates to more than a half million dead sharks every single year, just for their fins!" In January of 2003, Science magazine reported that Hammerhead and white shark populations along the East Coast of the U.S. have declined over 75% in the past 15 years, and many other shark populations have decreased by at least 50% in the same time period, largely due to overfishing and accidental harvesting on long-line rigs meant for other species.

Which then is the Predator and which is the Prey?

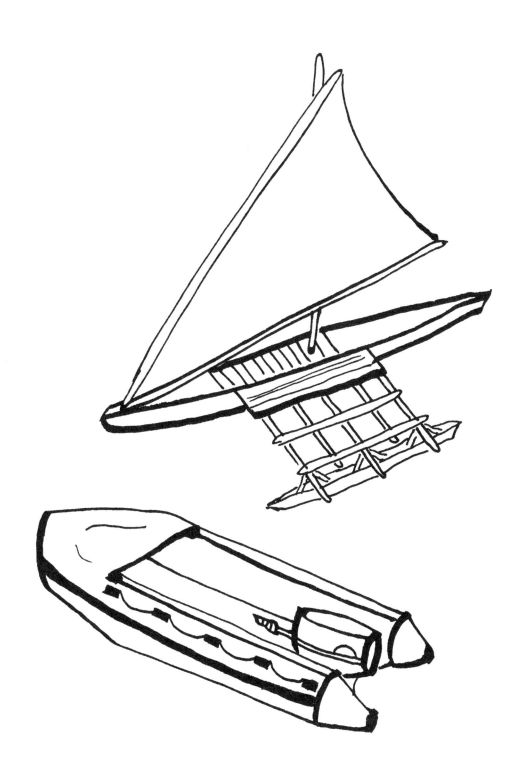

Halfway to Tonga

$\mathcal{J}$ don't *do* night-dives. You should understand that at the outset. Most of my diving experience has been in cold waters off the Southern California coast. There, even out at the Channel Islands, visibility tends to be limited, perhaps 60 to 80 feet at best, and at night those waters are dark.

Once, in the warm and relatively clear water of the Sea of Cortez, I did a night-dive. Nothing untoward or remarkable happened. But I spent the entire dive nervously looking around me, imagining all of the very large and very vicious creatures that were going to appear at any moment and attack me. It was no fun at all. So I don't do night-dives.

But this was such a simple plan, really. Practically foolproof. We would dive the channel at dead high tide. The channel is roughly 30 feet deep, 100 feet wide, and 300 yards long. At one end, it opens out into the tranquil lagoon of Fulaga (pronounced with an 'n,' as in Foolanga) where our live-aboard, the *Pacific Nomad*, was anchored. At the other end, it drops off precipitously at the outer edge of the reef wall into the dark blue depths of the South Pacific. The visibility was exceptional, at least 100 feet, and the water temperature was in the high 70s. The moon was full. High tide was supposed to be about 8:30 p.m. If we got in the water at 8 p.m. near the middle of the channel, we could make an hour's dive, letting the gentle, diminishing current carry us in toward the lagoon and then back out toward mid-channel. A crew member would follow our bubbles in *Tinny*, the little aluminum outboard-powered runabout.

We had dived the channel earlier in the day, riding the full-up incoming tide all the way from the outer dropoff into the still waters of the lagoon. It had been a marvelous joyride, practically effortless. The combination of the current and being weightless made it possible to relax completely, position one's body any which way—upside-down, sideways, sitting, backwards, whatever the whim of the moment—and watch the sights as they passed in review. Riding along with us were the turtles and fish, keeping their parallel pace. So you see, my guard was down. The spectacular beauty of the South Pacific reefs, the pristine, unspoiled nature of this very remote Fijian atoll, and the perfect diving conditions enticed me to make an exception. It was such a simple plan.

Ah, what fools we mortals be.

Four of us elected to make the dive. I would be diving with Jack, a long-time friend of ours from our local dive club back home. The other two divers were Bill and Joann, a couple from Seattle that we had met on the boat. After dinner the four of us suited up while the rest of the passengers, including Jack's wife, Vicki, and my husband, Jon, settled in for the usual evening's relaxation and partying. The crewman who would ferry us out to the dive spot got the walkie-talkie from Skipper Apete and we all piled into *Tinny*.

When we arrived in mid-channel, Jack and I got in the water first and settled quickly to the bottom. Jack would be doing photographic work for the dive so while he busied himself with setting up his strobes, I began exploring the sand and clumps of coral nearby. I noticed the current was a bit stronger than I had anticipated and it seemed to be heading outward toward the open ocean, rather than inward toward the lagoon. But I wasn't terribly concerned—I had been in stronger currents than this and, after all, it was at least close to high tide; we should have plenty of time to make the dive.

Jack began taking photographs, close-ups of the critters on a large mound of coral in mid-channel. As I moved from one rock across the sand to another, I observed that the current had become noticeably stronger. I grabbed hold of the rock as the current threatened to carry me past it and held on while I explored its crevasses for shrimp and other nighttime creatures. It occurred to me that it would be best to work our way up-current to avoid any chance of being caught too far out toward the mouth of the channel. But when I tried to move up-current to Jack to communicate this, I found that I could not make any headway.

As I clung to my rock, the force of the current became so strong that my lycra gloves were being shredded on the rough surface of the coral. I turned my head slightly sideways and the water almost tore off my mask. By now Jack had finished exploring that first clump of coral. I saw him relax into the current and let it carry him past me. He was unconcerned, apparently operating under the assumption that the tide was going in. That was, after all, what the plan had been.

By now the current was incredibly strong and I decided that it was time to abort the dive. I got to Jack and tried to pantomime that we were being carried outward. Failing that, I pointed at myself, then at him, then at the surface. Finally he agreed to ascend. By the time we reached the surface, we were at the outer drop-off and being carried rapidly out to sea. The channel opens outward in a roughly west-southwest direction, so I figured we were heading in the general direction of Tonga. I wondered idly how far it was from here to Tonga and how many sharks there might be in between. Fortunately, our crewman had spotted us and was quickly bringing *Tinny* to the rescue.

By the time we clambered back on board *Tinny*, we were roughly 200 yards out to sea. But then the little outboard roared to life and we motored back into the channel to find Bill and Joann. They popped to the surface just inside the dropoff and we motored quickly to them. Again, by the time we had them safely on board, we were 200 yards out to sea. *Tinny's* outboard roared to life and we began the trek back through the channel toward the calm shelter of the lagoon.

It was a beautiful, balmy tropical night. Now that we were well on our way back 'home,' we relaxed and compared notes about how strong the current was, jokingly speculating on just how far removed from high tide we actually were. *Tinny's* motor buzzed soothingly as we bounced across the choppy tidal waters and into the channel. Joann was shivering pretty badly from the breeze of our movement so we wrapped her up in our towels and continued chattering away, enjoying the beauty of the night and the after-buzz of excitement from our unexpected adventure.

Bounce. *Splat.* THUNK.

Three emphatic, rapid-fire sounds—and then silence. And once more, we were being carried by the tide, drifting out to sea, drifting toward Tonga.

The crewman had tried to shorten our trip by cutting across the top of the reef rather than following the channel all the way in. Unfortunately the reef is extremely shallow and *Tinny's* motor had just lost an argument with a coral head. Later, we found out that the impact had sheared the linchpin. For the present, all we knew was that the crewman was not having any success in his efforts to re-start the motor. After five or six tries, he gave up and reached for the walkie-talkie. No problem—we would simply call the boat and have them send out *Rubber Ducky*, the inflatable runabout.

But no one answered the call. We could hear, faintly, the voices of our friends on board the *Nomad*. The warm cheery sounds of the evening's festivities carried well on the tropical breezes. But apparently they could not hear our call. As first the crewman and then Bill fiddled with the walkie-talkie, Jack got out the biggest dive light we had on board and began to signal the old familiar *dot-dot-dot, dash-dash-dash, dot-dot-dot* distress signal. Over and over he flashed the pattern toward the *Nomad*.

As we fiddled and signaled and bobbed on the tide, getting closer and closer to the outer edge of the reef yet one more time, I looked up at the night sky with its huge full moon and large fluffy white clouds. We were all getting a bit nervous now. To allay our fears, we began the child's game of imagining patterns in the clouds. It was right after sighting the cloud-dragon that we heard the faint roar of an outboard. Within minutes we could see *Rubber Ducky* making its way out to us. We breathed a collective sigh of relief when we saw that they chose to stay in the channel rather than cutting across the reef. By the time they reached us we were once more out past the dropoff, on our way to Tonga.

As *Rubber Ducky* towed us slowly back to the *Nomad* we continued our cloud game, finding all sorts of wondrous creatures drifting and glowing, transforming and merging and re-forming in the magical moonlit sky above us. It was a charming distraction in a beautiful tropical night. But all of us were very relieved when we finally re-boarded the *Nomad* and were reunited with our friends and spouses.

Fiji is truly a paradise. I fell in love with it and left a significant piece of my heart there. I would return in an instant, especially to Fulaga if I could, and perhaps I will someday.

Just don't expect me to do a night dive!

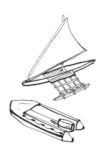

Spellbound

I drift suspended
In golden seaweed enthralled:
Leafy Seadragon!

Magic

The foam and froth of the sea leaped and sparkled beneath me and the wind whipped my hair in a wild dance as I leaned over the rail at the bow of the boat. Clearly visible in the waves, a pod of seven or eight dolphins streaked along with us, slipping smoothly and quickly from side to side. Every so often one of the sleek gray forms would spurt ahead of the boat, letting us know that it could easily out-race us—if it chose to. Then it would drop back to the bow wave once again, letting us know that it didn't choose to. The exuberance and effortless skill of these beautiful creatures has captivated me from the moment I shared my first joyride with them.

Over and over again across the years I have ridden at the bow, searching the waters for hours in hopes of another encounter. Often, a pod will change it course as we approach, deliberately angling directly toward us. A shout goes up, "Dolphins off the starboard bow!" and everyone on board scrambles for a place along the rail. We whoop and shout as the dolphins arrive and take their places under the bow. We cheer and clap and whistle as they leap and play in the foamy spray. They seem to delight in their games and we delight in them. All too soon, they tire of the game and cut away from us, returning once more to the course they had been traveling before they decided to intercept us. Exhilarated and laughing we return to the galley, savoring as long as possible another magic moment.

For divers there are many magic encounters, events so singular for their beauty and joy and rarity that they still shine in our memory years later, when all the other memories surrounding them have faded into faint shadows and whispers.

There was a dive that Jon and I made on Begg Rock, a massive underwater pinnacle near San Nicolas Island. It was one of the first times we had dived that spot and we were thrilled to find a small valley near the top of the pinnacle that was completely lined with white metridium anemones. Like lacy powderpuffs on 3-inch stems, they transformed the curved surface into a living carpet. We glided slowly through the valley and then turned left, heading down along a ridge that led away from the pinnacle. The water was cold and clear and intensely blue.

Suddenly we were startled to see a 4-foot long eel emerge from behind a large rock about 10 feet away. Its long brown muscular body was edged along its entire length by delicate upper and lower fins. Its massive head seemed too large for its body and its visage was magnificently ugly. This was no common moray eel—it was a wolf eel. The creature either did not see us or was not threatened by us, for it swam just below and ahead of us in the same direction that we were swimming for several minutes. As it glided along the ridge, its huge head showed no sideways movement, acting as a guide and anchor for the sinuous, undulating body and the fragile, rippling fins.

We were completely mesmerized. We had never before seen a wolf eel and we had never seen any eel free-swimming. We knew how rare this encounter was and we worked hard to keep up with the eel while it glided silently before us. Gradually however, the creature moved further ahead of us, growing smaller and smaller until it disappeared among the rocks that spilled down the side of the ridge. I looked at Jon, saw the marvel deep in his eyes, and reflected it back to him. We joined hands and continued along the ridge.

Although wolf eels are a rare occurrence, sea lions are very common in the waters of Southern California and provide many opportunities for magic. Their large brown eyes, whiskered snouts, and penchant for play remind me of eager puppy dogs. I even saw a pup do an excellent job at fetch one day. My friend Molly and I were snorkeling near the rookery on Santa Barbara Island when Molly felt a gentle tap on her shoulder. Turning around, she discovered a sea lion pup looking expectantly at her. On impulse, she grabbed a small piece of seaweed that was floating nearby and threw it a short distance away. To our great surprise the pup actually swam over, picked up the seaweed, and brought it back to Molly. She and the pup repeated this exercise three or four more times before the pup ducked back under the surface and swam away.

On another occasion, at the same rookery, I was teaching my 9-year-old niece how to snorkel and we gradually worked our way in toward shore. Chelsea was captivated by a large group of pups on shore that were apparently being given swimming lessons by three adults. The adults would trumpet to the youngsters who would then dash awkwardly into the water, splashing and barking and honking. They would swim around in the surf briefly and then head back to shore. Then they would repeat the whole exercise again. As we snorkeled closer, the pups turned their attention to us and swam out almost to where we were. Imagine this scene: Two human snorkelers treading water, their heads bobbing in the choppy waves, staring intently at a large group of sea lion pups, their heads bobbing in the choppy waves, staring intently at two snorkelers. The two snorkelers laugh and shout at each other excitedly, while the pups bark and honk and chatter among themselves with great animation. What fun we had that day!

Even adult sea lions love to play. One night, as we sat at anchor under a moonless sky, we spotted three large sea lions playing among themselves. At the time, the ocean was filled with what is called the Red Tide, a bloom of plankton that makes the water appear rusty red during the day. But at night, the same plankton produce a bioluminescent light when the water is agitated. We turned off all the lights on the boat and stood on the stern deck to watch our three visitors. As they moved through the water, each of them was outlined in a ghostly pale green glow that trailed off behind like a shimmering comet's tail. We watched entranced as they streaked through the inky dark water, chasing and tussling with each other. They performed an intricate high-speed underwater ballet for us, doing loops and twists and rolls, tumbling over each other and then streaking off in follow-the-leader formation, only to return within seconds to repeat the performance all over again. I do not know how long they played—it might have been 5 minutes or 25 minutes. I only know that we watched every second and even now, many years later, when I close my eyes they are playing still, painting their ghostly green swirls in the black depths of my mind.

Although these incidents have been very special, most of them involved us watching as the animals played—a relatively passive experience. How much more thrilling it is to participate and play with them! Once when we were diving the islands of Fiji's Southern

Lau group, we spotted a school of manta rays as we were waiting in the inflatable chase boat for the remaining divers to complete their dive. We had no air left and it was late afternoon—too late to return to the mother boat for another air-fill—so we popped into the water on snorkel and swam to greet the mantas. There were 6 of them in all, ranging in size from about 6–15-foot wingspans. All of them had white markings on their backs and one had lost its left wing-tip—it was blunt-cut about a foot back from where the tip should have been.

The mantas seemed to welcome us into their group; they cruised back and forth and around in circles as we chased and followed them. Jack had a camera and was trying to photograph the action, but the mantas would veer sharply away from him whenever his strobe lights flashed. Evidently they didn't like the bright flash, but other than that they seemed to really enjoy playing chase with us. They made no attempts to leave or otherwise avoid us nor did they threaten us in any way.

They soared slowly and gracefully, without effort, on their huge and powerful wings, while we had to swim as fast as we could to keep up with them. We stayed in the water with the mantas for about 45 minutes until it got so dark we could hardly see. Reluctantly, we clambered back into the inflatable boat and started back to our mother boat. As we headed out, one of the larger rays came up under the boat and bumped its back against the bottom several times, giving us a good bouncing. The animal could easily have capsized us if it had wanted to—it was clear that it did not intend us harm. I've often wondered what message it was trying to communicate to us; a playful farewell perhaps or maybe a request to come back and continue the games.

More than anything else, it is incidents like these that compel me to return to the ocean over and over again. The opportunity to see and play with creatures of such intelligence and beauty and power supplies a magic that keeps my sense of wonder and joy vividly alive.

Ocean Wild

Fierce wind: blue-black swells foam white.

The ocean wild roars

My heart on ocean wild soars.

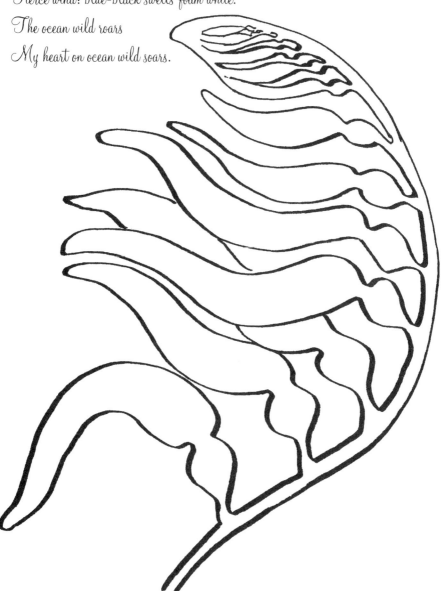

Just Another Perfect Day

It was being airborne that jolted me awake. In one of those instantaneous moments of all-comprehending cosmic consciousness, I knew that my bunk had fallen out from under me and that my body was about to follow suit. My cosmic consciousness also told me that the bunk was going to surge upward again at the same time and that the two of us—bunk and body—would very soon be reunited—very emphatically.

Oof!

After I refilled my compressed lungs, I sighed heavily, shifted my position so that I was wedged more securely in the bunk, and resigned myself to another brutal and sleepless night. I thanked Poseidon for giving me the foresight to take an anti-nausea pill before retiring.

Our boat was steaming "uphill" across the wide channel that separates Southern California's offshore islands from the mainland. "Uphill" means the boat is moving in the opposite direction to the swells. When the boat is moving rapidly and the swells are very large, this results in a contest between the irresistible force and the immovable object, neither of which cared the least little bit that precious cargo (i.e., me) was being brutalized in the argument. My husband, of course, was sound asleep. He can sleep through an earthquake so I wouldn't expect a bit of bumpiness on the ocean to disturb him.

When the engines finally stopped, I groaned, fell out of my bunk, and stumbled up the stairs to the stern deck. It was very dark and very rough. It was also very cold. Unbelievably, we were actually anchored at Begg Rock and there were divers on deck, suiting up for the first jump. I groaned once more and staggered into the galley to get a cup of coffee. The first swig was terrible. Fortunately, the second swig was even worse—awful enough to start the slow waking-up process. I balanced the styrofoam cup of foul black liquid carefully as I bounced awkwardly off a table, ricocheted off the nearby railing, and toppled a plastic chair on my trajectory back out to the deck.

To get out of the wind and keep my balance, I wedged myself into the open shower stall and surveyed the situation. I measured the size of the waves and the rough chop that animated their surface. I assessed the thickness of the dark cloud layer above. The skipper announced that we would make only one jump here due to the conditions before heading in closer to the island where—hopefully—the conditions would be more favorable. No one in their right mind would attempt this dive.

I began suiting up. A wetsuit is a full-length body girdle, designed to fit tightly enough to keep out all but a thin layer of water. They are thick, heavy, and cumbersome. I wrestled with mine heroically, sitting on a flimsy plastic chair in the galley. I jabbed one leg into the suit and started pulling, at which point the boat rolled emphatically to starboard and I, still in my chair, scooted all the way across the galley.

"We must be crazy," I said to Jon.

"Of course we are," he replied. "Would you like some help with that suit?"

"Nope—I'll be fine. Just stop rocking the boat, please!"

I made two more scoots across the galley before I was able to finish suiting up. In spite of the pitching deck, we fell into our well-rehearsed routine: Attach regulator to tank and check air supply; strap on diving knife and weight belt; clip gamebag to weight belt; sit down to slip into buoyancy control vest (to which tank is attached); check all hoses and gauges; don mask and gloves; grab fins; take a deep breath; and stand up.

"Yeah, right!" I exclaimed involuntarily as I staggered to keep my balance on the still-pitching deck with about 100 pounds of diving equipment strapped to my body.

"Are we having fun yet??"

Jon reached out to help stabilize me and then we started our short, but nonetheless challenging, walk from the tank bench to the gate at the side of the boat where we would enter the water. On most dive boats the gate is just an opening in the railing, about 3 feet wide.

The diver holds onto the rail with one hand while putting on his/her fins with the other hand and then shuffles flat-footed the last step or two to the edge to jump in. Piece of cake—as easy as falling off a log. Except that this boat was not designed for divers. The gate opening did not go all the way down to the deck—there was a foot-high piece of sideboard across what should have been the opening. A diver had to step up, place one foot on the narrow sideboard, and then swing the other foot up and over.

"Yeah, right!" I muttered once more under my breath as I watched the two divers ahead of us step up and swing up and over on their way into the water. "OK, if they can do it, so can I." The gray, choppy swells rolled ominously under the boat. I put my left foot up on the sideboard, took another deep breath, and swung my right foot up. Only it didn't go over. I hadn't made enough allowance for the 10-inch-long blade of my fin. The blade slapped the sideboard and my up-and-over movement became a headlong plunge into the sea. As I spluttered to the surface, gasping for breath from the shock of the frigid water, I realized that I had lost my right fin and my mask was hanging down around my neck.

The choppy water slapped my face furiously and the rolling swell carried me along the side of the boat. I grabbed at the swim-step as I went sweeping past it and managed to haul myself back on board, feeling at least as graceful as a beached whale. Swearing and muttering and shaking my head, I climbed up the ladder onto the deck.

"Hey, Judy, nice jump!" One of my dear friends shouted. Jon handed me my missing fin, which had flipped back onto the boat as I went overboard. Hiding my chagrin and embarrassment, I grabbed the fin and held it triumphantly aloft.

"Hah," I shot back, "I'll have you know that I was just practicing my new fin-flipping jump, and it was perfect!" Fortunately, this little white lie gave me the dispensation to sit out the dive, which I did in the warm comfort of the galley. When everyone was back on board, the skipper moved the boat in close to the island to take advantage of what little protection it could provide from the weather. Once more, Jon and I readied ourselves for the dive and I approached the gate feeling anxious but determined to conquer the damn thing. Which I did.

We descended 40 feet to the bottom and began exploring. The visibility was lousy; the water had a murky green appearance like very thin pea soup. It was difficult to see anything under those conditions but we continued swimming, hoping that the surge would abate and the visibility would clear up as we got closer to shore. Large rocks loomed up out of the murk and we navigated over or around them. At one point, I looked up to see a large dark bullet-shaped form hurtling directly toward me and a jolt of adrenalin exploded within me. I barely had time to form the thought "shark" before the beast was upon me, aiming straight for my facemask. But 3 feet away, it veered suddenly and sharply to the left and I realized as it disappeared into the murk that it was merely a sea lion, playing a common sea lion game called, "Scare the Bejeesis Out of the Divers." I swallowed vigorously to get my heart back down where it belonged and we continued on our course.

Soon we came upon a rock so large that we realized we would have to go way off course to get around it, so we decided to go up and over it. As we rose slowly, I kept my hand on the rock. This clever little trick accomplished two things: it ensured that I wouldn't be banged against the rock by the surge *and* it kept me oriented in the claustrophobic murk.

The next thing I knew, I was blinded by bright white foam and my head and shoulders were being slapped rhythmically and violently from behind. It took a few moments of struggling before I realized: This was no rock—this was the island! We had surfaced in the churning whitewater at the base of an enormous cliff. I looked straight up at 100 feet of solid rock and gulped involuntarily. I turned to look at Jon as the water thrashed around us like a gigantic washing machine. We both gave the thumbs-down signal simultaneously, nodded to each other, and plunged back down to the relative calm of the ocean bottom to work our way back to the boat.

As the crew raised anchor for the run home we breathed a sigh of relief; at least it would be downhill in that direction. Everyone crowded into the galley for lunch, laughing and swapping stories of the day's adventures. The cold waters and rough conditions had made us all ravenously hungry so we wolfed down large quantities of juicy cheeseburgers and an entire batch of freshly baked brownies. Occasionally a larger than usual swell rolled up from behind the boat, giving us all a rush as the stern of the craft rose and we picked up speed, surfing the great surge of water beneath us. We all had a mad scramble to grab the ketchup bottle, our drinks, and our plates to keep them from flying off the tables. We whooped and laughed as our chairs, acting like demonically-possessed bumper cars, carried us involuntarily and randomly around the galley.

Back at the dock, as I stumbled up the steep gangway with my gear, I realized that I had really enjoyed the day in spite of everything. Partly, it was the chance to escape from the ordinary and to spend an entire day without phones or newspapers or traffic or any other impediments of everyday life. Partly, it was the camaraderie of good friends. Partly, it was those outrageously good brownies. But more than anything, it was the opportunity to spend a few more moments in that other universe under the sea. I love the immense alien beauty and power of that world. I realize that if I am to continue to visit that place I must accept all of its moods and faces, both the good and the bad. And when I do, even a bad day becomes just another perfect day in paradise.

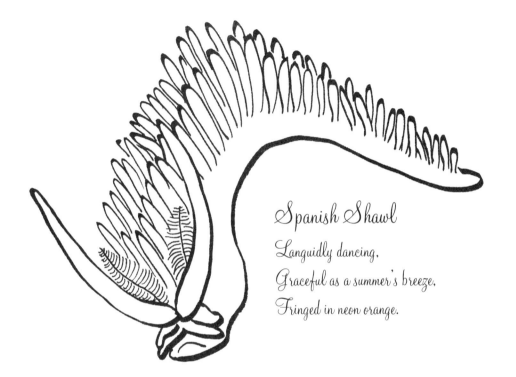

Spanish Shawl

Languidly dancing,
Graceful as a summer's breeze,
Fringed in neon orange.

Naked Gills and Sarcastic Fringeheads

"Must a name mean something?" Alice asked doubtfully.
"Of course it must," Humpty Dumpty said with a short laugh: "my name means the shape I am—and a good handsome shape it is, too. With a name like yours, you might be any shape, almost."

– Lewis Carroll

Jon's hand-motions signaled: Come over here and take a look. Curiously, his finger pointed not at the reef but at a spot several feet up and off the reef. I couldn't see anything from where I was, so I changed course and kicked over to him. Then I saw what had caught his eye: It was a tiny Spanish Shawl, less than two inches long, dancing languidly in mid-water, its bright orange fringe fluttering gracefully as the little slug's brilliant purple body twisted and gesticulated. As a form of locomotion this dancing movement made up in grace and beauty for what it lacked in speed and control of destination. I looked at Jon and nodded, seeing the smile in his eyes, and then we spent several minutes hanging weightless in the water, watching this beautiful creature as it danced and drifted slowly down, finally landing on a rock. It took hold of the rock with the flat bottom of its slug-shaped body and began gliding smoothly across the weedy growth looking for its favorite hydra food.

Intent as I was on watching the Spanish Shawl, I was somewhat startled by a quick movement off to my right. A mottled brown 6-inch-long fish had darted out from its protective crevice and was lunging at me, fiercely snapping its large mouth. I laughed to myself at the absurd bravery of the comical creature, with its disproportionately huge head. The silly little fringe-like structures above and between its eyes told me that this was a fish whose common name was the Sarcastic Fringehead.

Now, I can understand how the Spanish Shawl got its name—it does indeed look like a tiny colorful shawl when the animal does its watery dance. But what about that Sarcastic Fringehead? The Fringehead part is easy—it most certainly has tiny little fringes decorating its head. But I have never heard of a fish—any fish—uttering any words to anyone, sarcastic or not. A very peculiar name. I have searched through quite a few books on fish, looking for an answer without success. Let's look further at the naming of living things.

Both the Spanish Shawl and the Sarcastic Fringehead are common creatures in our California waters. The Spanish Shawl is a shell-less sea slug, closely related to the more familiar shelled marine snails. The Fringehead is one of many species of bony fishes, closely related to the fearsome sharks and rays whose skeletons are made of cartilage rather than bone. Throughout the years that I have been diving I have never ceased to be amazed at the endless variety of life within the sea. Life began in the sea and expanded beyond it only after eons of evolution. With three-quarters of our planet still covered by water, there are many more species that are water-based than are land-based. From the tiniest plankton to the enormous blue whale, the oceans teem with plants and animals of every conceivable size, shape, color, and function. Throughout our existence humans have observed, co-existed with, eaten, and been eaten by sea creatures. Scientists have spent centuries attempting to identify, describe, and catalog this wealth of life. They use a hierarchically organized scheme to categorize all living things according to their distinguishing characteristics. Just as we organize addresses hierarchically (continent, country, state, county, city, street, residence number), so are living things organized:

Phylum
 Class
  Order
   Sub-order
    Family
     Genus
      Species

The Spanish Shawl, for example, is classified as follows:

Phylum:	*Mollusca*
Class:	*Gastropoda*
Order:	*Nudibranchia*
Sub-order:	*Aeolidacea*
Family:	*Flabellinidae*
Genus:	*Flabellina*
Species:	*iodinea*

Well, I can guess what you're thinking at this point: You're shaking your head and wondering why those crazy scientists had to take a perfectly descriptive, wonderfully romantic name like the Spanish Shawl and turn it into something as tedious, obscure, and meaningless as *Mollusca Gastropoda Nudibranchia Aeolidacea Flabellinidae Flabellina iodinea*! It doesn't exactly flow trippingly off the tongue, now does it? But the mystery clears up rapidly if you know a little history, have some familiarity with ancient Latin and Greek, and can recognize similarities among different words. Centuries ago, Latin was the language of scholars, at least of the European variety. Thus, in the early 1700s when the Swedish naturalist Linne was working on his system for naming living things, he used Latin and Greek names. His own name in Latin was Linnaeus and the book that he published, *Systema Naturae*, is the foundation for today's scientific nomenclature. Knowing that, let's go back and take another look:

Mollusca is the Latin word for soft, and gastropoda is constructed from two words that mean stomach (*gastro*) and foot (*poda*). Similarly, *nudibranchia* means "naked gills." Now look yet again, this time at some English words that we use today, such as "mollify," "gastronomic," "podiatrist," and "nude." There doesn't appear to be a current derivative of *branchia* (meaning "gills"), but bronchitis is derived from *bronchia* (meaning "windpipe.")

The sub-order name, *Aeolidacea*, is a bit more challenging. The animals in this sub-order are named after the Greek god Aeolis, god of the wind. Perhaps they were given this name because their *cerata* (the finger-like structures such as the orange fringe of the Spanish Shawl) perform some of the animal's respiratory functions. My own guess however, is that it is based on the observation that these *cerata* move constantly due to the motion of the water around them, looking as though they are being blown and tossed by the wind. I have not been able to find an explanation or derivation for the family and genus names, but the species name, *iodinea*, is based on a Greek word meaning "violet-colored," giving us the word "iodine." Thus, putting together what we have learned, we have a soft-bodied animal that walks (crawls) on its stomach, has exposed gills that appear to blow in the wind, and a purple body.

We can perform a similar exercise with our little buddy, the Sarcastic Fringehead:

Phylum:	*Chordata* (sub-phylum *Vertebrata*)
Class:	*Osteichthyes*
Order:	*Perciformes*
Family:	*Clinidae*
Genus:	*Neoclinis*
Species:	*blanchardi*

The phylum name, *Chordata*, means "cord" and designates all animals that have a nerve cord. For those animals in the sub-phylum *Vertebrata*, this nerve cord is surrounded and protected by a bony spinal cord made of individual bones called vertebrae. The class name, *Osteichthyes*, is constructed from the Greek words for bone (*oste*) and fish (*ichthyes*). Although the word ichthyologist (a person who studies fishes) is not very common, most readers will recognize the root word for bone in such words as osteoporosis (meaning porous bone), and osteo-arthritis (meaning inflammation of the bone joints). The order name is a bit obscure, but appears to be constructed from the Latin and Greek words meaning "perch-shaped." I have not been able to find an explanation or derivation for the family name *Clinidae*, but whatever it means, the genus name then becomes a new (*neo*) whatever. The species name in this case is not based on Latin or Greek, but is rather the name of the person who first discovered the fish: S. B. Blanchard. Thus, our Sarcastic Fringehead is actually an animal with a nerve cord surrounded by a bony spinal column, with a shape that is generally similar to a perch and was first discovered by S. B. Blanchard.

While the scientific nomenclature may still seem somewhat obscure and cumbersome to most readers, it does provide a well organized and descriptive tool that scientists can use to help them study the more than two million living species of plants and animals that inhabit our planet. Like Humpty Dumpty, scientists insist that a name must mean something, whether it means a shape, a function, a color, the name of the discoverer, or some other characteristic. By organizing creatures into descriptive categories and sub-categories, it becomes much easier to understand how any particular species is similar to or different from other species. While common names are usually more "user-friendly," and at times even poetic, they lack the precision and the wealth of information contained in the scientific nomenclature.

But what about that Sarcastic Fringehead? For a common name, it is pretty obscure, albeit colorful. Well, it turns out that the word sarcastic comes from the Greek word *sarkasmos*, meaning "to tear flesh." Ah, now we're on to something! Perhaps this little fish was named for its fierce and aggressive nature or perhaps for the fact that its head fringe appears shredded or torn. Either explanation seems plausible, but for myself, I will always continue to hear in my head a fishy little voice, dripping with sarcasm, saying, "Hey Dumbo, quit spending so much time reading those stupid dictionaries and nature books and come back here where I can sink my teeth into those fat fingers of yours. I dare you!"

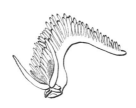

Immortality

The sea-wracked cliffs weep,
Spilling sad, slow tears of sand:
Even mountains die.

The Eternal Spiral

We shall not cease from exploration
And the end of all our exploring
Will be to arrive where we started
And know the place for the first time.
                    – T. S. Eliot

Webster's Dictionary defines 'remote' as: distant in space; far off; hidden away; secluded. Here is my personal definition:

Fly from San Diego to Los Angeles	0.5 hours
Fly from Los Angeles to Tokyo (cross dateline)	11.5 hours
Fly from Tokyo to Kuala Lumpur	7.5 hours
Fly from Kuala Lumpur to Kota Kinabalu	2.5 hours
Fly from Kota Kinabalu to Tawau	0.5 hours
Drive from Tawau to Semporna	1.5 hours
Boat ride from Semporna to Sipadan	3.0 hours

That's 22.5 hours of flying time, plus 4.5 hours by boat and van. Add to that 9.5 hours of sitting in airports and 27.5 hours spent in two hotels along the way, and the grand total is 64 hours in transit. That's more than two and a half days and one-third of the distance around the world. My husband Jon and I left home on Saturday, August 8, 1992 at 6:30 a.m. and arrived on Sipadan on Tuesday, August 11, 1992 at 1:30 p.m.

The goal of this long trek, Sipadan, is a tiny island off the northeast coast of Borneo. A leisurely 40-minute stroll along the beach will bring you full circle around the flat little island with its dense rainforest crown. If you stand anywhere on its beach and look around, Sipadan appears to sit alone in the world, floating in isolation in the middle of an ocean that stretches unbroken from horizon

99

to horizon. In the mythology of the Eastern Woodland Indians of North America, the world was originally a vast empty sea. Earth was created when Turtle dived down into this sea and brought up some mud from the bottom. She carried the mud on her back and, as she swam, it grew larger and larger until it formed land. Turtle Island. The Earth.

As Jon and I walked along Sipadan's shore, the warm salty smell of the sea mingled with the rich dank smells of the jungle. The white sand of the beach was marred only by our own footprints and the only sounds were the ceaseless rhythms of the waves, the exotic calls of the jungle and shore birds, and the incessant background buzzing of cicadas and other jungle insects. Truly, we thought, we are alone in the world. Then we saw the small wooden sign, barely visible among the mangroves which border the forest, dividing jungle and beach: "504," it read. A turtle nest, carefully counted and marked. We stopped to pay our respects but kept well clear of the precious spot.

Sipadan is renowned for its populations of turtles, mostly the large Green turtles and the smaller Hawksbills. A sturdy hut near our diving camp on the north side of the island houses the local Wildlife Station personnel who patrol the island every day to locate and mark all the nests so they will not be disturbed. Every hatching of a nest, with the concomitant scramble of tiny shells and flippers down the sloping sands and into the welcoming waves, is cause for celebration as these turtles struggle to maintain their own in the face of constant encroachment by humans. No one is allowed to roam the beach beyond the camp at night, which is when the turtles come ashore to build their nests.

Halfway down the east side of the island is the hermit's hut, a typical wooden box on stilts with a steeply canted thatched roof and an open front porch. It is set back against the jungle and we kept close to the ocean as we passed, not wishing to disturb the old man who resides there. He appeared to have company; four or five men were sitting on the porch, talking quietly. Partway out on the beach was a small wooden platform without walls and a young man was sitting in it. We speculated that the platform was perhaps a lookout shelter, used for patrolling the beach. We'd been told that the hermit is a native who has lived on the island most of his life, and that by local rules and customs he has the hereditary right to collect and eat or sell up to 80% of the turtle eggs. Turtle eggs are very popular in Malaysia and we found many of them for sale in the local markets on Borneo.

Having completed our circuit of the island, we once more returned to our diving camp. There are actually three camps, all packed closely together on the narrow north end of the island. Our camp, run by Borneo Divers, accommodates up to 40 divers at a time and has a staff of 27 people. The other two camps appeared to be of similar size, making the island population about 200 at any given point in time. The calculation startles me. Two hundred people living on 30 acres begins to approach the population densities of the civilized world that we had spent 64 hours traveling to remove ourselves from! And indeed, the apparent remoteness of the island is caused only by our limited ability to see beyond the horizon, beyond the surface. Sipadan does not float by itself in an empty sea—it is an underwater mountain soaring almost half a mile from the ocean floor to the surface, the last outpost in a chain of sea-rooted mountains called the Sulu Archipelago. These mountains stretch southwest from the island of Mindanao in the Philippines to the island of Borneo, dividing the Sulu Sea to the north from the Celebes Sea to the south. It sits near the center of the Southeast Asian island nations of Indonesia, Malaysia, and the Philippines, all of which are members of ASEAN, the dynamic, rapidly growing economic "Tiger of the Pacific." The daily sounds of hammers and saws that we heard on Sipadan as the diving camps expanded were being echoed in the native water villages that we visited on Borneo, where whole new subdivisions marched on stilts out into the rivers and bays, and in the thriving metropolis of Kuala Lumpur, where the Petronas Towers and other lesser skyscrapers soar into the intense blue sky. (Over the course of the 9 years since this trip, the ASEAN Tiger experienced a major economic meltdown, the impact of which was felt worldwide, but from which both the Tiger and the world have largely recovered.)

And yet, sitting on the bench at the end of the pier, sipping a gin and tonic as the sun moved slowly down toward the western horizon, watching the flocks of golden Imperial pigeons as they returned to the island for the evening, listening to the gentle lapping of the wavelets on the pilings, it was easy to maintain the illusion of living at the remote ends of the earth. Our life there was very simple: sleep, eat, dive, eat, dive, eat, relax, sleep—a pleasurable ritual which we repeated every day for a week.

The camp was comfortable, if somewhat primitive. It consists of a spacious dining hall (with bar), a large and well-organized dive center, a lodge for the staff, two single huts, and nine double (i.e., 2-room) huts. We occupied Room 3, in the second double hut that is next to the lodge, very close to the dive center. The huts are basic native-style wooden structures, built on stilts with a floor of raw planks spaced a half-inch apart, plywood walls with a shuttered glassless window opening on each side of the door, and a 16-foot-high pointed thatched roof. Each room is about 10 x 12 feet, with two single wood-frame beds, each with a mosquito-netting tent covering it, one dresser-sized wooden cupboard for storage, and a small "end table." The upper portions of the walls are slatted open for ventilation. There is a single neon light fixture, a ceiling fan (which we kept running all the time), and a 220-volt outlet for charging strobes. Behind the huts is a shower building, consisting of six shower stalls with solar-heated water. Further back in the jungle is a large "outhouse" with three men's and three women's flush toilets. There is no fresh water source on the island; all drinking water is brought over from the mainland and other water needs are supplied by a desalination plant, which was broken during our stay and could not be repaired until the necessary spare part arrived from the mainland. Thus, we showered all week in brackish water pumped from within the bowels of the island. Other than the solar power used to heat the water, power for the camp is supplied by a generator, the constant hum of which is muffled effectively by the amount of jungle vegetation between it and the camp. The generator is powered by gasoline, as are the motor-driven dive boats that ferried us to our dive sites twice a day.

It was the diving, of course, which had brought us there. The island of Sipadan represents only about one-sixth of the area at the top of the mountain. The remainder of that area is a shallow reef, shaped much like an arrowhead, with its point toward the south. From this flat summit, the mountain plunges precipitously straight down for 2,000 feet. Most of our diving entailed floating along the sides of this mountain, varying our depth by adding or expelling air from our buoyancy compensators. The shallow top reef and the sheer mountain walls house an unimaginably rich biomass, spectacular both for its diversity and its sheer numbers.

For our first boat dive, we jumped in the warm tropical water at Staghorn Crest on the east side of the reef and drifted south with the current to South Point. We began at a maximum depth of 85 feet, but spent most of the 50-minute dive in less than 60 feet. What we saw was incredible: a group of about eight white-tip reef sharks hanging out together, numerous other single white-tips, all about three to five feet long, eight turtles, a black-tip reef shark, two different kinds of lionfish, dozens of very large barracuda, hundreds of hard and soft corals, anemones, sponges, and crinoids in endless variety and every conceivable color. We floated in and out and through multiple hoards of reef fishes which darted and schooled all around us. We drifted past a cleaning station beneath a 5-foot-long table coral, where a large triggerfish hung motionless with its mouth open as a tiny cleaner fish nuzzled in and out, seemingly indifferent to the threat posed by the monstrous teeth surrounding it.

On and on we drifted, the massive wall of the mountain offering up its glorious beauty for our eyes and souls to marvel at: an enchanted Fairyland. Visibility wasn't as crystal-clear as we had expected—it varied from about 50 to 70 feet—but the bountiful life teeming around us more than made up for that small disappointment. About halfway through the dive, we drifted over a small bench area that jutted out from the side of the mountain. Its surface was nothing but masses of mangled, dead coral branches, ghostly white bones heaped in violent disarray, a stark and jolting contrast to the pristine beauty and vitality of the rest of the reef.

Lunch gave us the opportunity to relax and refuel, and to meet the camp mascot, Morris the Monitor Lizard. He came slinking across the beach in front of the dining hall, as he did every day, his tail and claws leaving a very distinctive trail in the sand as he moved along in his slow—and very dignified—manner. His body was about a foot long and his tail almost doubled his length. He was dark gray in color with subtle white markings. His tongue was long and forked and constantly darting out and back, out and back. He appeared to be "tasting" the air and sand as he walked. Delightful.

Our afternoon boat dive took us to the west side of the reef/island/mountain, drifting southward from Hanging Gardens to Lobster Lairs. Whereas most of the reef wall is merely vertical, the aptly named Hanging Gardens is actually undercut, so the abundant soft corals there really do hang downward. It is a bit disorienting to feel like one is upside-down in addition to being weightless. We saw perhaps a dozen turtles on this dive, including a Green with a 4-foot-long shell resting peacefully in a shallow cave in the wall. In one spot there was an upwelling of colder water mixing with the warmer surface water; the visual effect was very strange and distorted, rather like trying to look through animated wrinkled glass.

Even with two boat dives per day, there was plenty of time for snorkeling and beach diving along the northern end of the island in front of the camp. On one of our snorkeling excursions around the pier, we came upon a veritable army of parrot fish, all busily munching away at the chunks of coral strewn about: recycling it by turning it into sand. The sound of their munching was quite audible even from 40 or 50 feet away. On another excursion, I was charged by a 3-inch-long triggerfish apparently in an attempt to scare me off. He was quite brave and insistent, coming at me fiercely every time I got too close to his rock until I finally took the hint and moved on. I checked in on him every other day or so during the week and he was always there, always defending that same rock.

On our second evening, as we sat on the pier sipping our pre-dinner cocktails watching schools of fish "boil" as they feed (or are fed upon), we saw a single 4-foot barracuda shoot suddenly out of the water at full speed. It skipped four or five times across the surface of the water directly in front of the lodge just beyond the drop-off and then disappeared under the surface again heading west. In hot pursuit close behind the barracuda was a good-sized triangular fin slicing the surface of the water. We weren't able to tell who finally won the race because they both disappeared under the surface. What an exciting interlude! Shortly afterwards, we noticed on the horizon to the north a trio of obviously military ships steaming slowly eastward. One of the camp staff explained that they were Malaysian Navy gunboats, patrolling the waters for pirates. They passed in review each evening and became a familiar sight to us, both reassuring and oddly disturbing.

The next day, after a full day of diving and snorkeling, we napped briefly after dinner and then met in the dining hall with our guide from the Wildlife Station. Under his watchful eye and expert guidance we were permitted to walk the beach that evening in search of turtle nests. The moon was huge and full in a cloudless sky and the tide was out—a beautiful, balmy night. We had flashlights with us but we didn't really need them as we walked down the east shore. About two-thirds of the way down we found a fresh turtle trail. They are very easy to identify; the turtle's body carves a wide, continuous groove from the water up to the mangroves and the flip-pers leave a series of short depressions on both sides of the body track. We waited on the beach while our guide went back into the brush to investigate. There was indeed a turtle but she was still trying to decide where to dig. We continued walking down to the lighthouse at South Point, then came back to the turtle track and waited on the beach until about 10:30 p.m. We could hear clearly, above the rhythmic sounds of the waves and the whispers of the wind, the crackling and rustling of the bushes and the scraping and falling of the sand as she labored to dig her nest.

The guide checked on her again and came back to tell us that she was now laying eggs and he led us back into the brush to see her. She was a Green, with a shell roughly three and a half feet long. Our guide estimated that she was about 70 years old. She lay on the sand over the deep hole she had dug, and though she was clearly aware of our presence, she seemed to be in a world of her own as she dropped her eggs one by one into the nest. Female turtles have much smaller and shorter tails than the males, which enabled us to see the eggs as they dropped. About five feet away was another shal-lower nest, very close to a mangrove bush. She had apparently first started digging there but had run into too many roots, so she had moved out further into the small clearing where we found her. We were able to talk quietly, shine our flashlights, move around her, and even take a few flash pictures, apparently without disturbing her. I was intrigued to see a distinct trail of "tears" flowing from her eyes, just as I had heard of. Seeing her was a very touching, compelling, and fascinating experience.

We walked back to the camp in the moonlight—silent, elated, and afraid. Turtles are such shy, gentle, elusive and graceful creatures and our very love for them may be driving them away and destroying them.

On our morning dive the next day, we went to Turtle Patch which was protected from the strong swell that had been kicked up by a storm that had passed through during the night. We saw only a few turtles on this jump—it was mostly a pretty wall with lots of fish. In one spot we were able to swim among an enormous swirling school of yellow and white butterfly fish along with clouds of yellows and other darker fish—all of them only five to six inches long: an enchantment of darting, shining jewels all around us. I felt like Alice floating in Wonderland.

As we worked our way along the wall we heard a series of three very loud explosions that really frightened me. I had no idea what it was but I had visions of a gunboat overhead, chasing pirates and dropping depth charges on us. We could feel the sound as a concussion on our chests. After we surfaced, our Divemaster explained that it was probably the sound of the natives dynamiting fish on the next island over, which was 10 miles away. Dynamiting is a very popular method for fishing; the natives mix powdered sugar and fertilizer, both of which are readily available, to form an explosive. The mixture is apparently quite volatile and unpredictable, resulting in frequent injuries, but they continue to use it. On questioning, the Divemaster confirmed that such explosives had been used occasionally on Sipadan before the dive camp was established, which explained the devastated reef areas we had seen. Dynamiting is no longer permitted on Sipadan, but how long will it take those devastated reefs to rebuild themselves?

The days passed in a leisurely, rhythmic dance: sleep, eat, dive, eat, dive, eat, relax, sleep. We lived in our bathing suits, day and night. Dressing for dinner meant putting on a (reasonably clean) T-shirt over one's bathing suit. Every moment of every day brought new sights and new experiences. By the end of the second day of diving my mind stopped trying to find new superlatives to describe what I was seeing. I reverted to a pre-verbal existence: My mind lived in my eyes and my ears. One evening, I deliberately focused on sounds; the jungle at night sounded like hundreds of tiny squeaking hinges against the backdrop rhythm of the waves and the constant hum of the generator. In the evenings, the geckos up in the eaves chirped periodically. At night, lying safe within my mosquito-net cocoon, I could hear the rats shuffling and skittering along the floor of the hut, looking for leftovers. Throughout the day I could hear kingfishers squawking and scolding and the multi-level up-and-down, up-and-down trill of the sunbirds. Back in the jungle, the pigeons cooed constantly.

Eventually, of course, the dance must end. On our last afternoon of diving, we worked our way across the northeast tip of the reef at Barracuda Point and then south to Coral Garden. This was a longer dive than usual—65 minutes, ranging from 65 feet to 10 feet. Divemaster Adeline had promised to show us a rare pink leaf-fish if she could find it again. Luck was with us; it was in its customary spot, but hidden down among some big chunks of dead coral. It was indeed hot pink! I tried to find a way to get my camera in close enough for a shot, but couldn't, so Jon pulled one of the chunks of dead coral out of the way. With that, I managed to get one shot before Adeline came back to get us, motioning for us to catch up with the group. I think she was upset that we disturbed the fish and I felt a rush of guilt. With macro work especially, where you work so close to the reef, it is difficult to avoid doing damage to the reef and to its inhabitants, even unintentionally, and here we had deliberately dismantled a protective shelter just to get a better photo angle. I vowed to be more careful from then on.

After dinner, Jon and I sat on the pier quietly watching the sea and the stars. The evening was lovely, soft and full of magic. And the stars were beautiful—in the clear, intense black of this remote sky, the Milky Way was so bright and dense it looked like a cloud. We saw a meteor flash by and what we guessed to be a satellite blinking its course across the night. There were frequent flashes of lightening on the horizon to the northwest. I wished that I could wrap the night and the ocean up in a scarf and take it home with me. I knew it was going to be terribly hard to leave the next day.

Throughout the boat ride to Semporna, and the van-rides from Semporna to Tawau to Sandakan, the images of Sipadan that were burned into my mind kept replaying, a graceful and watery counterpoint to the scenes of the road and jungle that were now surrounding us. We were on the mainland of Borneo, in Sabah, its northern-most state. Sabah is called "The Land Below the Wind" because the typhoons generally follow a storm track that runs north of here, rarely hitting Sabah itself. The natives call Sabah the "Sad Paradise" because it is so beautiful and because the typhoons sometimes strand them here when they are trying to reach their homelands.

The area between Semporna and Tawau is mostly plantations; predominately oil palms, but also some coconut palms and cocoa plants. I saw one sign for a rubber plantation but it was old and worn—perhaps it is no longer an active plantation. The soil is a bold orange-red and the profile of the land is flat with a few low hills. There were some small patches of old rainforest and a number of areas, still smoking, that had been cleared in the traditional fashion: slash and burn. One local newspaper article indicated that the increase in "slash and burn" activity was causing increased soil erosion and runoff, resulting in a spreading blight of murky "green water" that was clearly visible in the photograph accompanying the article. The green area reached out from mainland Borneo almost as far as Sipadan. (In the fall of 1997, severe air and sea pollution due to out of control "slash and burn" activity in Indonesia made world headlines, destroying hundreds of thousands of acres and threatening to choke over 70 million people living not only within Indonesia but its ASEAN neighbors also).

Our goal when we reached Sandakan was a visit to the Orangutan Center. Orangutan is a Malaysian phrase; *orang* means "people," and *utan* means "forest": the 'wild men' of Borneo. The Sepilok Orangutan Center is a rehab station situated on the edge of the rain forest. Its purpose is to rehabilitate orphaned and pet orangs so that they can return to their natural habitat, free and wild again.

The rain forest is huge, tall, moist, and rotting. Its heavy, fetid air is filled with a constant cacophony of sounds. As we walked on a wooden plank path beneath the great canopy of trees we encountered a number of macaques, both long-tailed and pig-tailed varieties. One beautiful female pig-tailed macaque was sitting placidly next to the path with her baby in her arms. We stopped to watch her and take pictures and she seemed to enjoy the attention. In fact, she would turn to face the camera as though she were proudly showing off her sweet-faced little baby. We went on to Platform A where we could watch the rangers feeding the orangs, but it was extremely crowded and we couldn't see much. Many of the tourists were Malaysians with their children.

After visiting the small nature museum and watching a short film about the Center, Jon and I returned to Platform A. By now there were very few people there and within a short time a young (probably two or three years old) male orang came swinging along the "highway" rope strung in the trees. He dropped off the rope near the platform and ambled slowly over toward us, munching on a large leaf. He crawled up on the platform and just hung out with us for about 15 minutes. We had been instructed not to touch the animals because we could transfer diseases (colds and flu and such) to them and because the goal of the Center is to wean them from their attachments to humans. So we didn't touch, but the little guy and I were face to face. He posed for the cameras and spent as much time gawking at us as we did at him. He had such a sweet and intelligent face that it is easy to see why people adopt them as pets. Unfortunately, cute little baby orangs grow rapidly into adult orangs that are human-sized but much more powerful and much less sociable, at which point they are either condemned to confinement in a zoo or abandoned in the jungle without having learned the skills they need to survive there.

The next day, we visited a crocodile farm a short drive out of town. They had dozens of crocs, both large and small, all lying about in their ponds, so completely motionless that they looked dead—monumentally ugly creatures. In a pen by herself there was one 70-year-old female croc with a horribly distorted snout, curved severely upward, with no teeth. Her disfigurement had been caused by the fact that she had been raised in a cage that was too small for her; it gave her no growing room. She was monstrous—horrid—but I couldn't help feeling sorry for her; it is a terribly cruel thing to do to a living being.

Our flight from "The Land Below the Wind" carried us to Kuala Lumpur (KL) in time to celebrate our 18th wedding anniversary. KL is very much a modern city with a population of about 3 million, complete with skyscrapers and freeways and traffic jams. It feels and looks very similar to Los Angeles so we felt very much at home there. The Shangri-La Hotel sent an air-conditioned Mercedes with an Indian driver to fetch us from the airport. A half-hour ride brought us to the hotel—a very classy and posh 5-star 28-story hotel in the middle of the city. It has an elegant feel very similar to the Biltmore in L.A. although it is much newer and its decor is simpler than the ornate old-world-style Biltmore. The staff is very competent and friendly and helpful and the building is beautiful: high ceilings, spacious rooms, lots of marble and brass, and thick carpeting.

I took a leisurely shower and then did make-up, hair-dryer, and curling iron for the first time since we had left home two weeks earlier. We ate our anniversary dinner at the hotel in their continental restaurant, Lafite: crystal and silver, fine china, waiters in sparkling white dinner jackets and white gloves. Their guest chef for two weeks was from San Francisco so we ate California cuisine. What a contrast this was to our little thatched-roof, rat-infested hut on Sipadan!

We finished dinner about 9 p.m. and took a cab over to Chinatown to Jalan Petaling—the Night Market. Little knock-down stalls lined the street for about six blocks, swarming with people, both locals and tourists. It is very much like our flea markets: hundreds of T-shirts, cheap watches, sun glasses, belts, wallets, tie-dyes, and the occasional stall of semi-precious stones and Indian jewelry, including an old skull-cap (probably monkey) with silver decorative overlay in the Tibetan style. There were also lots of food stalls. The vendors are much like the shopkeepers in Tijuana: noisy and joking, cajoling their potential customers with "Perfect for the lady" or "Your size shirts here—King Kong size" for Jon. We wandered through the whole market area, stopping to buy some T-shirts (of course).

As the evening progressed, we sat down at one of the food stalls to have a beer and watch the crowds swirl around us. I was fascinated to see, at a large table nearby, a half-dozen Chinese men drinking beer, laughing, and playing a very animated game of paper-scissors-rock, a game that I had known since my childhood back in Pennsylvania. It was unmistakably the same game; I recognized the hand symbols for paper, scissors, and rock. But here I was, four decades older and half a world from my roots!

On our long journey home the next day, and often over the years since then, my mind fills with a swirling kaleidoscope of images from this trip: the overwhelming abundance of Sipadan's reefs, the vast richness of the rain forests, the vitality of Malaysia's cultures and peoples. These images are also sharply punctuated by the broken bones of dead coral, the tears of the turtle, the sweet face of a young orphaned orangutan, the smoking ruins of burned jungles, and the twisted snout of a hideous old crocodile. Having changed the face of the First World beyond recognition, we humans now seems bent on doing the same to the Third World. Our power appears limitless and nature is far too fragile to withstand the onslaught. Even its most remote corners bear the scars of battle.

But then I remember the Chinese men at the table and their simple child's game. Rock smashes scissors, scissors cut paper, paper covers rock in an endless cycle of destruction and renewal, force and counter-force. The fragile paper has a power of its own and brings the game full circle. Perhaps so does the fragile reef and the vulnerable rain forest too. Fish convert coral to sand and coral convert microscopic plants into mountains which crumble slowly to sand once more. The dance of transformation is timeless, eternal, and we humans are merely a small part of that cycle. We ride on Turtle's back as she spins her slow waltz through time and space, obeying the fragile power of the universe.

(Postscript: In the 1999 edition of the Travelin' Diver's Chapbook, the reviews indicated that the number of dive operations on Sipadan had increased to five. The next year, of course, Sipadan became internationally infamous when a group of tourists and several resort staff were kidnapped and held hostage. About a year later, a cyclone hit the island. The 2003 edition of the Chapbook includes only one report on the island, dated January of 2002. This report says that the visibility was 15 to 30 feet, there were no big schools of fish, and, in reference to Coral Gardens, it says, "Coral Rubble might be a better name.")

> *Nothing abides. Thy seas in delicate haze*
> *Go off; those mooned sands forsake their place;*
> *And where they are shall other seas in turn*
> *Mow with their scythes of whiteness other bays.*
> LUCRETIUS 96-55 B.C.
> (W. H. Mallock translation)

Dialog

Many worlds from home,
A frog squirms, a woman grins—
Laughter needs no words.

Shore Leave

*C*ognitive dissonance. That is "psycho-babble" for the alarm ringing, or maybe even screaming, in your head when you become aware of two or more ideas that clash. A beautiful woman wearing a flowing silk evening gown with her mud-encrusted combat boots. The angelic smile on the killer's face as he squeezes the trigger of his .44 Magnum. A fish no bigger than your fist ferociously bumping its tiny nose against the face-plate of your mask.

Or, a slender teen-aged Malaysian boy casually donning his leather racing gloves as he stands beside a battered old van with bald tires. Uh—that would be the van that we are to ride in. Yes. And that would be the driver of the said van.

We were stranded in Tawau, a little town on the northeast side of Borneo. Fresh off the boat from a week of glorious tropical diving, we had arrived at the Tawau airport about 3:00 p.m. No sooner had we unloaded and settled in to wait for our plane than we were informed that our flight to Sandakan had been cancelled. The staff from Borneo Divers who had brought us here just shrugged, said they couldn't do anything about it, and promptly left us on our own. The next plane scheduled to Sandakan was the following afternoon. Totally unacceptable. We were all on a tight schedule, trying to squeeze as much as possible into the few remaining days that we had to spend in Borneo. If we had to wait 24 hours for a flight, we would miss our visit to the orangutan sanctuary in Sandakan—an experience I was especially looking forward to. And of course, there was the added enticement of checking into a real resort hotel and being able to take a long leisurely shower in fresh water. Oh God—was I looking forward to that! I had been showering all week in brackish water, which left my skin constantly sticky and my hair stiff enough to stand up like the 'do of a demented witch. I wanted that shower and nothing was going to keep me from getting it that evening. Nothing.

There were eight divers in our group. We all ganged up on the airline agent and insisted (in our best "Ugly American" fashion) that he had to do something. Find us another airplane. Not bloody likely in a tiny town like Tawau, a measly rancid scrap on the extreme fringe of civilization. Then we'll take the bus. Nope—there is no bus service to Sandakan. After a half-hour of our massed verbal onslaught, the agent agreed to go out in search of some form of ground transportation for us. What he found was a Toyota van, blue and battered, with VERY bald tires.

The driver and two other local boys worked rapidly to load the van. Divers traveling in tropical climates typically don't pack much in the way of clothing. All you need is a couple of bathing suits, one or two pairs of shorts, and enough t-shirts to ensure that you have a relatively clean one for dinner every evening. One pair of sandals will get you through even an extended trip because you throw them in your empty suitcase when you arrive and don't fish them out again until you are ready to head back to civilization. Ah—but then there is the dive gear: heavy-duty dive fins, lighter-weight snorkling fins, booties, mask, snorkel, lycra skin for very warm water, tropical weight dive suit for somewhat cooler water, regulator, an assortment of gauges, dive computer, weight belt, buoyancy vest, dive light, spare straps, a tool kit for repairs, and one large beach towel: enough to stuff a very large suitcase per person. And there is also the underwater camera equipment: usually one or two cameras, with one or two strobes each, and enough film to stretch from one ocean to the next: enough to stuff another good-sized suitcase. Jon and I had two large suitcases (our dive gear), one medium sized suitcase (our cameras), and two small suitcases (clothing, toiletries, basic emergency medical supplies, plus our stash of Oreos and peanut butter). The other six divers had equivalent loads.

After watching the boys carefully stack most of the large pieces of gear into the back of the van (with the largest pieces perched precariously on top of the smaller ones), we began cramming ourselves into the seats. It was extremely cozy, to say the least. Ginny and Emily and Bill were in the far back seat, all three positioned immediately under Big Ugly Green—the monstrous hard-sided suitcase containing my dive gear that formed the summit of the mountain of luggage behind them. Bill had to rest his feet on top of a large suitcase on the floor, which extended forward beside the bench where John and I sat. On the bench in front of us were Patti and Paul and one of the Malay boys, who had only half a seat to sit on. In the front seat were the driver, the other boy, and Jon. We stashed our smaller bags underneath the seats or held them in our laps. We were packed in so tight that we could shift our positions only by carefully choreographing and coordinating our movements with those who sat beside us. I don't know what the other benches were like, but the one I was sitting on had very old, tired padding that did not disguise in the least the real, hard wood underneath. *Oh well,* I thought, *it's only 300 kilometers (about 180 miles) to Sandakan. It'll be uncomfortable, but no big deal.*

After we all settled in, our young driver got behind the wheel, carefully adjusted his spiffy all-leather driving gloves, and off we went. It was 4:00 p.m. and the road was well-paved. We figured we should be in Sandakan by 7:00—in plenty of time for dinner. The Malay boy on the bench in front of me was riding with his head hanging out the window, looking remarkably like the family dog, eager and innocent and excited. As we were leaving Tawau, I pulled out our Lonely Planet guide book to look at the map of the area: we would be traveling northeast for about a third of the way, then turn north for the remainder of the trip. Then I looked more closely: the map showed a large gap in the road going north, a gap which was roughly a third of the total distance from the turnoff of the Tawau-Semporna road to the turn-off into Sandakan. Uh-oh. I showed my fellow passengers and asked if they had maps that we could compare. Nope. I stared at the map. The map stared back at me with a toothless gap-in-the-road grin. Probably just a glitch in the printing process, I thought. Happens all the time in these cheap mass-produced paperback books.

The road was two lanes, one for each direction, and there was considerably more traffic than I would have predicted. I had a clear view of the road ahead from my seat, which I began to regret within a very short time. Our driver drove as fast as he could, passing slower vehicles and playing chicken with the oncoming traffic. He was actually quite skilled and didn't push the envelope too far, but

I finally convinced myself that I would be much happier if I didn't look out the front when he was passing someone. Instead I entertained myself with enjoying the scenery. We rolled along through miles of plantations at first, which gradually gave way to the dense native rainforest. Through the open windows, the thick humidity enveloped us with the rich fetid smells of moist earth and rotting vegetation. After making our left turn off the Tawau-Semporna road, the rainforest dominated, scarred only occasionally by small areas of slash-and-burn clearing. Some of these patches were very recently cleared, giving forth tendrils of wood smoke that smelled at once familiar and vaguely exotic. We were on a gradual ascent now, weaving our way up through a rugged mountainous region. As we reached higher, we had some beautiful views of mountains and valleys and at one point caught glimpses across a large bay to the east in the distance. We passed through a couple of tiny villages, but mostly saw only scattered houses—the usual huts on stilts.

There was one town, Kota Kinabatangan, which was sizeable enough to trap us in a traffic jam. We were forced to stop and then creep forward ever so slowly, even though there was not another car or truck in sight. The problem was the dozen or so cattle which were standing and/or laying in the road, casually in ones and twos, as though they were in their own pasture. The smells of fresh manure mingled with the now familiar earthy and vegetal smells of the rainforest. In addition to the cattle, the other thing that slowed us down was the potholes scattered about in the dirt road in great variety and large numbers.

Yes, I said dirt road. It turned out that the strange anomaly in the guidebook map was an indication that this section of the road was still under construction. We had left our lovely, smooth paved road far behind and were now traveling on an extended dusty washboard sprinkled liberally with small craters. The cattle jam gave us a brief respite from the bouncing, jarring vibration of our journey, but once we cleared the village, there was nothing to keep our driver from proceeding apace. My rear-end went numb. I remembered—quite vividly—the bald tires. My fellow passengers and I exchanged meaningful glances. We engaged in intermittent bouts of jokes and light patter, bravely keeping up the facade of "The

Happy Divers on Their Grand Adventure." My rear-end progressed from numb to number.

Then it got dark. Jungle dark. It began to rain: heavy sheets of water smashed against the windshield and battered the metal shell of the van like a great steel drum. I looked out the front and all I could see was a large smear of mud and a hint of windshield wiper-blades. Occasionally, when we hit a nasty bump, the headlights would turn off momentarily. I began to have visions of the bald tires blowing out in a pothole, scattering our broken bodies around in the voracious brown mud. On the brief stretches of paved road, I had visions of those bald tires planing on the slick wet surface.

We bravely continued to joke and exchange meaningful glances as we droned on through the storm and the night. The young boy with his head out the window was by now a very soggy-looking puppy. He also looked like he was checking the tires periodically. Occasionally we passed isolated houses, most of which were dark shadows in an even darker forest, though there were some in which electric lights burned, pinpoints of light piercing the wet night. On and on we drove, bouncing from pothole to pothole, sliding through muddy flats, our headlights blinking off and on as though startled by the black wetness assaulting us.

The rain finally stopped and we were past the construction area, so we relaxed a bit. We finally reached Sandakan just before 9:00 p.m. We had been on the road for almost 5 hours, with not a single stop, without even being able to shift our sitting positions more than an inch or so in any direction. We were stiff and sore, ravenously hungry, and tremendously relieved to have made it through that dark and stormy night intact. We checked into the Ramada Renaissance as quickly as we could and went down to the coffee shop to eat. Janet, from the tour company, came to see us to make arrangements for the next day's tours and to tell us that our flight from here to Kota Kinabalu was in doubt. The runway was cracked or had a hole in it, or some such. Probably a rogue pothole that wandered in from the road we had just traveled. She said she would try to make alternate arrangements for us, if necessary. By this time it was far too late for that fresh-water shower I had been looking forward to so desperately, so I went to bed sticky one more night. I slept soundly, dreaming of orangutans in driving gloves, nimbly dodging great potholes amid torrents of steaming black coffee. In the morning I took the longest, most luxurious shower of my life.

When I sat down for breakfast, I suddenly realized how terribly sore my tailbone was. It was so painful that the only way I could tolerate sitting was to adjust my posture to a constant tilt, rather like the leaning tower of Pisa. Fortunately at the time, I was blissfully ignorant of the fact that I would have to sit like that for the next 18 months before the pain finally left. After a savory breakfast of Murtabak (Indian bread with curried pea sauce), we had an hour or so before the bus was to arrive to take us to the orangutan sanctuary, so we wandered down to the market. There we saw the native women ensconced in their stalls, selling fruits and vegetables, both strange and familiar, spices, ginger, toiletries, breads and cakes, dead chickens and live peeps, beef hooves, and hundreds of fish— all kinds of fish, including several angelfish, sharks with their fins cut off, live crabs, and beautiful iridescent tuna. The strong mixture of animal, vegetable, spice, and sewer smells created a strange and rich perfume, unique and heady. As we strolled through this visual and olfactory kaleidoscope, one old woman in particular caught my eye. She was sitting on the ground, her mouth stained orange by betel nuts, her black eyes following, seeking intently to connect with me. I met her gaze openly and directly as she raised her hand, holding up a small, perfectly round frog. As soon as it registered on me what I was seeing, I burst into delighted laughter. Her weathered orange mouth and jewel black eyes laughed in response, crinkling her face into pools of concentric wrinkles, and then she let the frog go. It squirted a short stream of liquid to express its indignation and then hopped off in a huff. The memory of that old woman with her frog sparkles in my mind's eye—a gloriously quirky moment that alone was worth every pothole my poor tailbone had suffered.

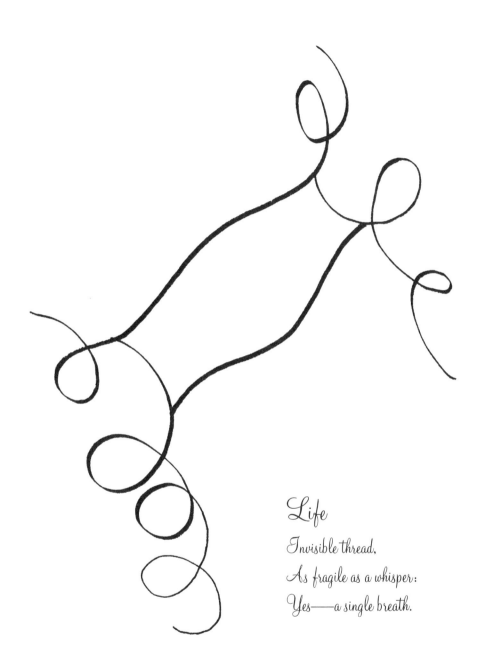

Life
Invisible thread,
As fragile as a whisper:
Yes—a single breath.

A Single Breath

The shouting was muffled, almost inaudible, but there was an intensity, an urgency, that could not be ignored. Someone was running along the port side, bare feet pounding on the deck. I turned around to look out the galley window just as Robb vaulted over the bow railing, plunging into the cold morning sea. He was dressed only in his wetsuit—no fins, no mask and snorkel, no tank. Something was very wrong.

Mike, one of the deckhands, threw a life-ring overboard with a long rope attached and a few seconds later began hauling the rope back along the port railing toward the stern. "Grab the ring!" he shouted. "Hang on! We're right here—we'll pull you in!" Another deckhand named Steve raced down the ladder at the stern and stood on the swim-step, his body tensed and straining.

From the water, a voice panicked and pleaded, "Oh God, please help us! She's not breathing!"

Robb and the two deckhands came up the ladder carrying a diver, the neoprene-clad body sodden and limp and awkward, arms and legs flopping lifelessly. Behind them came another diver, his terrible pleas ripping through his fear-choked throat. "Please, please help her! She's not breathing. This can't be!" As he pulled off his mask and hood, I recognized him. His name was Alex. With a jolt, I realized that the lifeless body now lying prone on the rear deck had to be Jamie.

I had met her only the night before, as our boat left the harbor for the start of our 3-day Labor Day weekend dive trip. I had noticed her sweatshirt with the Indiana University logo and we had spent some time comparing our experiences at our common Alma Mater. She had majored in music, I in Psychology. Her stay had been almost 15 years after mine and yet there was a bond. She was excited about the trip, never having dived the Northern Channel Islands before.

Her dark eyes crinkled as she smiled and I eagerly shared with her my love of these islands.

Robb and the two deckhands worked rapidly, literally cutting Jamie's wetsuit off her body. Her skin was as gray as the fog, her lips a ghastly unnatural blue. I watched her chest intently for any sign of movement, for the tell-tale rise and fall of living, breathing lungs. She was still. Without any hesitation, the two crew members began CPR; Mike began breathing into Jamie's mouth as Steve began rhythmically compressing her chest. Over and over again they repeated the sequence: compress, compress, compress, breathe; compress, compress, compress, breathe. One of the passengers, Darlene, moved forward from the crowd and volunteered to help. She was a nurse. She began checking for a pulse: "No pulse," she reported.

At this, Alex collapsed and screamed, "Oh my God—I've killed her—I've killed my sister!"

The rest of us stood back watching helplessly, stunned beyond comprehension, unwilling to believe what we were witnessing. Someone said with quiet intensity, "Come on, Jamie, breathe!" The rest of us channeled our wills in response: "Breathe, Jamie, breathe!" As he forced his weight down on her chest, Steve shouted at her, "Come on, Jamie, stay with us!" Hope dwindled and shriveled within us as we watched her gray, unresponsive form.

But at last, when the stillness had almost completely engulfed us, Jamie's chest and stomach muscles contracted convulsively, forcing a great, horrible, wrenching, gurgling cry from within. She threw her head to the side to eject the sea from her lungs and she began to breathe.

The sudden reversal from the profound stillness of death to the piercing cry of a newborn wrenched us from bleak despair to elation. "Yes!" We said, triumphantly. "Breathe, Jamie!"

But with each breath came that same horrible animal cry, a sound so extreme, from a place of such desperation and fear and pain that it shredded my heart. She was fighting now, each breath one more terrifying step back from death, the enormous black fathomless depth that had taken her from us. As she fought, we fought with her. Blankets appeared and were wrapped around her. We breathed with her, cried with her, shouted at her to stay with us, to breathe. Every second of that battle was distorted into an eternity and it seemed that we were caught in some vicious time-warp eddy, end-lessly repeating the same cries, the same battle, the same intense urgings. But gradually her cries softened and her quiet interludes lengthened. Color was returning to her skin and lips. Darlene reported that her pulse was stronger now, and steadier.

Released from our spell, we began to search for explanations and answers. Off to the side, Eric, the Skipper, was talking with Alex, trying to find out what happened. We heard only parts of the conversation and we shared our own observations with each other. Gradually, a coherent story emerged. Alex and Jamie had completed a 75-foot dive and were hanging on the anchor line at about 15 feet, doing a safety stop. After the customary 5-minute stop, Alex sig-naled to Jamie to ascend to the surface. But when he reached the surface and turned around to look for her, she wasn't there. He looked back down the anchor line and saw her, still at 15 feet, still hanging on the line, but with her regulator out of her mouth, appar-ently unconscious. He quickly went back down, brought her to the surface, and yelled for help.

We tried to make sense of it all. Had they dived too deep? Ascended too quickly? Was it a case of shallow-water blackout? Had she clung too tightly to the anchor line and experienced an embolism from the heavy surge? Any of these things were possible—we didn't have enough information to come to any con-clusions. Failing that, we tried to estimate how long she had been without oxygen. A minute or two for Alex to discover her and bring her to the surface, another minute or two to get her on board. Perhaps as long as four minutes without oxygen—enough to cause brain damage. We whispered the possibilities and prayed that we were wrong.

As the crew and Darlene continued to work with Jamie, the Skipper put the rest of us to the task of preparing for the arrival of the Coast Guard rescue helicopter. The deck had to be completely cleared. All the tanks, all the dive gear, ropes, floats, buckets, spears—everything that wasn't nailed down—had to be moved into the galley. In imitation of the old "bucket brigades," we formed a line from the deck into the galley and began hefting gear from hand to hand, stashing everything as neatly as we could until the galley was filled and the deck was bare. The fear and adrenaline surging within us made each tank and weight belt and gear bag another demon to be dispatched and expelled. As we hefted and stashed, vanquishing Jamie's demons, the remaining crew began dismantling the skeletal PVC structure that rose above the deck and served as a storage rack for kayaks and a small motorized skiff.

Finally, the deck was naked, except for the three people huddled around the pile of blankets that was Jamie. As the helicopter hovered over the deck, we packed ourselves as tightly as possible into what little space remained in the galley. The water beside the boat churned furiously under the chopper, its huge blades roaring rhythmically above the gleaming white fuselage with its heroic red stripe. Engulfed by the enormous sounds and pummeled by the fierce winds, we watched in breathless silence as a man in an orange jumpsuit was lowered to the deck by a rope. A second rope lowered a steel-framed stretcher. With the precise and disciplined movements of a well-trained soldier, the muscular, crew-cut Guardsman directed the crew to help him secure Jamie on the stretcher. Slowly, expertly, they lifted her up to the hovering chopper. After a brief discussion with the Skipper, the Guardsman hooked himself back into his harness and was hauled back up to Jamie and his waiting teammates.

Then, the helicopter was gone and we were left to face the emptiness of the deck, the silence of the sky, and the unknown fate of a diver who had come back from the dead. The remainder of our trip was blessedly uneventful. We dived on beautiful reefs, floating weightless in our beloved ocean, but the weight of Jamie's life hung over us. We shared wine and laughter over dinner and snuggled in our warm bunks at night. But the laughter masked our fears and the warmth of our bunks could not keep the chill of Jamie's gray skin from our minds.

A month after the trip, one of the passengers called to let me know that she had just spoken with Jamie on the phone. Unbelievably, she had recovered fully and rapidly with no lasting ill effects whatsoever. With that marvelous news, my mind returned once more to that weekend and I struggled to comprehend the enormity of what I had witnessed. I recalled a dream I had many years ago, a dream in which I was trapped underwater and struggled frantically against the urge to breathe that swelled ever stronger within my breast. Finally, I could no longer resist the power of that urge, that most primitive of instincts, and I breathed. I remember with great clarity the feeling of the cold water invading and filling my lungs and the shock of knowing that with that breath I was dying. But that was a dream, from which I awoke. For Jamie it was not a dream, but a terrible reality. Since that day, every time I stop to listen to my own breathing, I realize once more how fragile that simple act is and how profound: The only thing separating life from death is a single sacred breath.

Salt

The wilderness waits.
Salt swirls and flows in currents—
Nurturing new life.

The Eye of the Beholder

Beauty is altogether in the eye of the beholder.
— Margaret Wolfe Hungerford

I've never seen a Boojum tree before. It looks like an overweight flagpole that's been on a bender and came back sporting a 4-day growth of scruffy stubble. Impassively, it stands sentinel beside Mama Espinoza's mailbox in the glaring sun as we eat great quantities of succulent fish tacos in her café, washing them down with pitchers of fresh lemonade. Boojums are endemic to this part of Mexico, the long finger of the Sonoran desert that thrusts southward as the Baja Peninsula, a parched and jagged remnant ripped violently from the mainland eons ago by the San Andreas fault.

After lunch, with ice cream cones in hand, we wander down the street to the Mercado. Inside, a glass display case greets us in an unexpected way: lined up neatly on its two shelves are rows of glass jars of various sizes, each filled with a clear liquid in which something dead floats, tranquil and oblivious to our gawking. There are quite a few rattlesnakes in assorted sizes from cute and tiny to large and menacing, interspersed with scorpions, tarantulas, lizards, and even a horned toad. The haphazard collection of jars bounces around in my mind, triggering a random assortment of memories. I remember the horned toad that my brother and I kept as a pet when we were kids. We'd take it out to our rose garden and watch it burrow into the dirt until only its nostrils were left uncovered. There it would sit for hours, apparently happy and content. I remember an unnoticed rattlesnake warming itself on a rock pile in a forest clearing and my brother's quiet warning that had stopped me from stepping on it. And I remember a scorpion, small and still and golden, that I found in the women's restroom at the lab where I work back in San Diego. My colleague Mike had been upset that the janitor had killed it—it would have made a fine companion to the pet scorpion he already had at home.

Across the street from Mama's place is the open yard of the local construction supply store, its entrance gate guarded by the great bleached skull of a gray whale. The mass of its brain case matches Jon's mass as he hunkers down beside it and its nose bones are every bit as long as his 6-foot 4-inch frame. I have time to snap his picture before our tour-guide calls us back to our bus to continue our southward journey. We still have another 360 kilometers to travel today.

Leaving El Rosario, Highway 1 turns eastward away from the Pacific coast, running down the middle of the peninsula for about 200 kilometers before bending westward again to meet the coast at Guerrero Negro, our destination for the night. As our bus lumbers south, the desert scenery flows past my window, the near expanse racing backward while the farscape seems to stream forward, keeping pace with us. I have watched a similar illusion many times out on the ocean as our dive boat steamed across the channel. As then, I let the motion and the illusion sooth me, emptying my mind and opening a great channel through my eyes. The rhythm of the hills and the rocks, the cactus and the shrubs, the earthen rusts and tans and greens and golds sing and dance in my awareness and I dream of the whales.

Guerrero Negro marks the dividing line between Baja California and Baja California Sur; a line which is also the northern boundary of the Desierto de Vizcaino and the one million acre Vizcaino Biosphere Reserve. Within the protective shroud of the Reserve and its great desert lie two lagoons that open onto the Pacific: Laguna Ojo de Liebre and Laguna San Ignacio. It is these two lagoons that are our ultimate destination. We have come to experience the winter breeding grounds of the California Gray Whale. It is late March and the breeding season has nearly ended. Most of the adult males have already begun their long migration up the coast to their summer feeding range in the Bering Sea. Many of the females have also departed, some of them newly impregnated. They will return to these lagoons next winter to give birth and nurture their babies in the warm and tranquil waters. Most of the females who have given birth this winter are still in residence, nursing and waiting while their offspring gain sufficient size and strength to make the 6,000 mile trip north.

Guerrero Negro, both the town and the smaller lagoon just north of Laguna Ojo de Liebre, are named for the *Black Warrior*, a whaling ship that sank in the lagoon in 1859, a scant two years after Charles Melville Scammon, captain of the whaling ship *Boston*, discovered the lagoons. For decades thereafter, the birthing lagoons became a deathtrap and a slaughterhouse for the whales. The whalers called them "Devil Fish," because of their power and the ferocity with which they defended their young when attacked. From an estimated population of 30,000, the grays were hunted nearly to extinction in the latter half of the 19th century. But they have made a remarkable comeback in the last hundred years, with their population now estimated at about 26,000 and in February of 1972, something magical occurred. Two Mexican fishermen in San Ignacio lagoon found their panga surrounded by hundreds of whales. For an hour they were afraid to move for fear of disturbing the whales and provoking an attack like the one that had killed several fishermen a few years earlier. Then, for reasons that he cannot explain, Pachico Mayoral reached out his hand and touched the whale that hovered beneath his boat and a new era in human-whale relations began. In the 30 years since then, word has spread, and the number of "friendlies" visiting the lagoons in the winter has steadily increased. Whale-watching has become a popular tourist attraction at both lagoons, and here we are to see for ourselves if the stories are true.

Our way to Eco-Tours Malarrimo in Guerrero Negro takes us through a portion of the great salt marshes that surround the lagoon, supporting a host of birds: ospreys, great (white) egrets, great blue herons, Brant's geese, avocets, godwits, curlews, and other shore birds. I even see a white pelican along the way, but my favorite by far is the reddish egret. Its coloring is extraordinary: a soft gray-blue body gradually shading into a smoky-rust neck and head.

These same salt marshes also support Exportadora de Sal, S. A. de C. V. (ESSA), a large salt-exporting corporation now owned by Mitsubishi. ESSA exports about three million tons of salt per year from this operation and our journey takes us through the salt ponds that have been created to produce this huge amount of salt.

Some of the ponds we are seeing have been abandoned due to chemical problems. All the ponds have a strange look to them—great shallow squarish-shaped depressions with water that is a green-aqua color so intense it looks plastic. The ponds are decorated liberally with irregular ridges of salt, running like tiny crystalline mountain ranges across the shallow water. There are no birds anywhere near the ponds. According to our guide, the salt concentration in the ponds is so high that the water is as thick as glue.

Near the water's edge we pass a 30-foot high mountain of salt awaiting its journey across the ocean to unknown destinations. I'm awed by its gleaming white mass. Because I have Addison's disease, I am acutely aware of how important salt is to human life. My body has lost the ability to retain sodium and, without proper medication, I would rapidly become dehydrated and my entire nervous system would begin to malfunction. I would slip into a coma and then die. While many Americans suffer from too much salt in their diets and are instructed by their doctors to reduce their salt intake, I have to be careful to take my medication daily. Sometimes I joke about craving salt so much that I even salt my potato chips, which is only a slight exaggeration. The mountain of life-giving salt now before me makes me smile, even as I wonder what effect ESSA has had on the whales' mating and nursery grounds.

Eco-Tours Malarrimo is very well organized, dividing the 36 of us up into four groups for the four pangas that will carry us out onto the lagoon. The panga Jon and I are assigned to is the *Malarrimo*. The other three are the *Susana*, *Tonina*, and *Leviathan*. The day is overcast, cool and windy, making us glad that we've brought our Warm Wind dive jackets along. We head out toward the mouth of the lagoon, which is much larger than I had imagined it would be. Our journey takes us "up-hill," heading into the wind and the chop, and we travel at high speed, so the ride is wet and bone-jarring. Even at high speed, it takes us over 15 minutes to reach the vicinity of the mouth of the lagoon, but finally we arrive and our driver abruptly drops the motor to low speed for whale-spotting. There is a swell rolling in from the open ocean, but it's running only about two to three feet. It's the three-foot high wind-blown chop on top of the swell that is the challenge. We all keep our seats as well as we can while our driver skillfully maneuvers us among the splashing peaks and slick valleys as we search the waters for gray whales. We had seen several dolphins on our way out, which is always a thrill for me, and I want very much to believe that it is also a good omen for us.

Even though the end of March is very late in the season, the Malarrimo tour guide has told us that there are still about 300 mother-calf pairs in the lagoon. I'm afraid to hope for too much, but the voice in my mind speaks over and over again: '*Come, Ballena Madre, and bring your beautiful Nina to greet us.*' Each of us calls out as we spot a heart-shaped blow, or the graceful slow-motion curve of a back with its distinctive knuckles. There are whales all around and we see three or four other boats in the distance. *Come, Ballena Madre, and bring your beautiful Nina to greet us.* Our driver suggests we sing to call the whales. Monica and Elena, two young women from Italy, immediately begin a lilting *la-la-la*, interrupted occasionally by very animated Italian chatter. The rest of us join in intermittently, but it is the Italians who keep the song going.

No more than 20 minutes into our search, someone shouts excitedly and points off to starboard as two dark forms move majestically toward us. It's a mother and baby! Suddenly they are with us and seven passengers rush to starboard. I am seated mid-ship on the port side, so I dutifully stay there, leaning as far to port as possible as we had been instructed, acting as ballast, assuming that some of the others will move back and let me have my turn. (Rule #1: to hell with being polite and following the rules when there are whales to be petted.) The mother rises first, bringing her massive rostrum up out of the water and blowing with an authoritative *whoosh*! I watch her two nostril slits flare open as the fine spray erupts, and then squeeze closed again before she slips softly under the surface. I can see clearly the large patches of bleached gray barnacles and pale pink sea-lice that give her dark skin a mottled appearance. The pair then hover on the starboard side, partly under our boat. I feel a gentle *bump-bump-bump-bump* under the bow. And once more: *bump-bump-bump-bump-bump*. Very soft. Very gentle. I have no fear. Somehow I'm certain that it is a greeting. The baby rises to the surface, rubbing her rostrum up against the side of the boat. She doesn't have very many barnacles as of yet, but already her blowhole is decorated with a thick pink band of lice. I notice she has a well-healed scar on her left side, a strong and straight three-foot long white line that runs from a foot or so behind her blowhole, down and forward, ending behind her eye and mouth. 'Baby Slash' I name her. Of course, I have no idea whether this is a 'she' or a 'he', but I can't bring myself to call such a beautiful animal an 'it', so 'she' it is.

I catch a glimpse of Baby's full length and am startled to realize that she is almost as long as our 18-foot boat. When born, these calves are about 15 feet long and weigh close to a ton. She could easily swamp us. I remember reading that the adult cows reach about 45 feet in length, longer than the full-size bus that brought us here, and weigh 35 tons—about equivalent to 10 good-sized elephants. A "Devil Fish" larger than a bus filled with wild elephants hovering directly under our little 18-foot panga as we bob on the cold and choppy surface of the sea. Yet, still I have no fear.

Mother and Baby glide beneath us and emerge on my side, Mama rising first, rolling on her side to get a good glimpse of us, and then submerging to support Baby Slash as she greets us and rubs against the boat. I touch Baby's rostrum, then her back behind her blowhole, being careful to avoid the very sensitive blowhole itself. Her skin is soft and smooth and rubbery, and glistens blue-black. Her breaths are much smaller and quieter than her mother's, a soft and sweet spray on my face.

Over and over again we dance the same dance, Mama and Baby Slash moving slowly, deliberately, beneath and around our little boat as it bounces in the rough waters, and the eight of us scrambling clumsily over each other to see and touch and photograph. At one point, Baby Slash comes swelling up to the surface beside me, her full length stretched out with her tail flukes pointing forward beyond the bow. Instinctively, I rip my sunglasses off just as Baby rolls onto her right side. I gaze directly into her left eye and know beyond a doubt that she is returning my gaze. Even in such a young animal there is a strong presence, a sense of an intelligence there, open, seeking, and receptive. *You are so beautiful*, I think to her.

Finally, Mama and Baby turn and glide off toward the *Susana* and the *Tonina* about a hundred yards away. Our driver points our panga out toward an area further south where a number of spouts are visible. I look at my watch: we have spent a full 40 minutes with Mama and Baby Slash. The exhilaration crackles among us.

We all laughingly attribute our success to the Italian singing and continue to scan for more whales. They are everywhere. All around us. We witness spy-hops and breaches, hear the whoosh of their breath and see over and over again the heart-shaped vapor of their spouts. We watch intently as one group of about 6–8 whales gather tightly together, touching each other, rolling over leisurely en-masse, flippers and tail flukes rising out of the water seemingly at random. One passenger wonders whether we are witnessing a mating session, but it seems too late in the season for such activities, and although we look as hard as we can, we catch no glimpses of the wonderfully named 'Pink Floyd' that would confirm the presence of an amorous male. Later, we are told that this was probably a group of mothers and calves nursing. Nursing in groups is a common behavior. Each baby consumes about 50 gallons of milk per day and the milk is 50% fat.

I glance at my watch again: we have been out watching for almost 2 hours—soon it will be time to return to shore. I watch as a mother-baby pair approach us from starboard again and I'm thrilled to recognize Baby Slash. Once more, she and Mama surface to rub and be petted, first on the starboard side and then again on the port side. But this time it's a very brief encounter and then they are gone. It was almost as if they knew it was time for us to depart and just came to say good-bye.

Our driver hands each of us a baggy containing a tuna salad sandwich, a banana, and a little candy bar and produces our choice of soda from his cooler. As we wolf down our lunch, he guns the motor and points our bow up-lagoon toward the dock. Although we're heading 'down-hill' with the swells, there is still a substantial chop that makes our ride back almost as kidney-jarring as the ride out had been. When he increases the speed even more, I look around and see one of the other boats just off our starboard stern, also running at full throttle. It's a race to the finish. We hold onto our hats and lunch bags and everything else that isn't nailed down as the wind and the water and the great long sandbars rush past us in a blur. I love speed and a high-spirited contest, but I get a little concerned when I see the dock approaching us rapidly with no sign from the driver that he is even remotely considering cutting back on the throttle even a teeny tiny little bit. I'm certain that we're going to run full-speed right up onto the beach and not stop until we crash into the van. But apparently he knows what he's doing and stops us perfectly, right at the dock. I let out a triumphant whoop—our *Malarrimo* has won—and then we all shed our vests and scramble out of the boat to greet and swap stories with our friends from the other three boats. The biggest news is that Sam kissed a baby. It had spy-hopped right next to where she stood in the boat, so she just leaned over and kissed it. What a delight!

Later that afternoon, we travel the remaining 144 kilometers south to the little oasis town of San Ignacio, where we will stay for the night before our next whale-watching excursion. It is less than a two-hour drive and I think all of us could fly there without the bus, fueled entirely by the joy and wonder we have experienced with the whales.

After so many hundreds of kilometers of dry desert, we are quite unprepared and thoroughly delighted at the sight of a veritable sea of palms before us as we crest the last hill. We arrive at the oasis about 5:00 p.m., stopping for photos at the river before proceeding into town. In the warm golden light of the late afternoon, the native fan palms and imported date palms fairly glow and the water, with its backdrop of volcanic hills, seems magical. Our next stop is the town square, centered with huge spreading shade trees, anchored by a well-preserved and wonderfully ornate Jesuit church, and decorated all around by tiny shops. The general store on the corner is a treat—rows of bottles of a liqueur called Guaycura Damiana, in large and small bottles as shapely as the Venus of Willendorf, tables piled high with T-shirts, freshly baked date bread, in addition to an assortment of general goods. Along the way to the hotel we pass the blackened remains of a very old vineyard that had been planted by the Padres when they arrived, to provide sacramental wines.

This evening, our tour guides instruct us in the fine art of doing tequila shooters, complete with limes and salt. We learn the traditional toast: "Salud, amor, dinero, y el tiempo para disfrutarlos": "Health, love, money, and the time to enjoy them." Well spoken! Once we are good and toasty, we sit down at a long table for a feast of traditional "finger foods." Afterwards, as we cross the inner courtyard on our way back to our room, we hear frogs in the swimming pool, singing songs of love to each other in the darkness.

The next morning, we leave the hotel right after breakfast, traveling now in four vans run by Kuyima Ecotourismo, one of the local whale-watching outfits. It's about 35 miles to the lagoon, but the trip takes almost 2 hours because the route is a very rough dirt road, wash-boarded and full of rocks and pot-holes. The particular area we are now passing through is volcano country—there are volcanic cones all around us and the desert floor is peppered with various sorts of volcanic rocks. We settle in to enjoy the scenery along the way. Much of it is similar to what we've already experienced, but this is the first time we've seen "bush ocotillo," a close relative of the ocotillo we know from Anza Borrego. I remember once, years ago, sitting in my window seat on an airplane as we flew over the great desert expanse of the Southwest. I was enthralled by the symphony of form and color that moved beneath us. The stranger in the suit sitting next to me commented, "Boy, it sure is barren down there." He meant well, I'm sure, just trying to make conversation to pass the time away. But it was obvious that he'd never had or taken the time to discover the beauty and life that fill the desert. I muttered something vague and polite and then went back to my window gazing. For me, the desert and the ocean are the same. Vast and alien, one must work to pierce the opaque surface, that deceptive barrier that seems so lifeless. But once within, one is immersed in a world that swells with life and beauty. I experience a fundamental simplicity, a peace that reaches my center, and that brings me back over and over again—to the desert or the ocean. It matters not. It seems so appropriate that the lagoons we are now visiting are wrapped in desert vistas, the liquid fingers of the sea entwined with the sandy fingers of the desert. What more fitting of a place could the whales have chosen to celebrate their lives and nurture their young?

When we finally arrive at Kuyima's camp, we are welcomed by Carlos, brother of the camp's founder, Jose de Jesus Varela Galvan. He tells us that we will be going out in 6 boats and that, because of the exceptionally low tide, we will have to wade out to board the boats, rather than using the little stair-steps that they usually use on shore. Before we board, Carlos explains the rules: only a certain number of boats are allowed on the lagoon at one time and all must be properly licensed. The speed limit is 3 mph when near the whales and the boats cannot chase the whales or approach any closer than 100 feet: the boat must let the whale approach it. No touching the whales too near their eyes or on the blowhole, flippers, or flukes because they are very sensitive there. He reminds us that actual contact with the whales is rare: only about 30% of visitors have such an experience, so he advises us to just relax and enjoy, and remember that it is called a whale-*watching* excursion, not a whale-*touching* excursion.

After picking up a safety vest from the pile on shore, we all take off our shoes and socks, pull up our pant-legs as best we can, and slosh slowly through the shallow water out to the waiting pangas. Our panga is *Kuyima-1*.

Although San Ignacio Lagoon is much smaller than Guerrero Negro, it is still a very large and long body of water and our destination is again out near the mouth. The day is even more windy than yesterday had been, though the chop seems not quite so large—perhaps because the surface area of the lagoon is smaller. Nevertheless, we are running at a strong angle to the wind and chop, so we get pretty well soaked from spray as we bounce along, and once more we are very glad to be wearing our Warm Winds. The journey out is about 15 minutes long and takes us along the salt marshes of the eastern shore of the lagoon—great for bird-watching, but I'm not really focused on birds. I want to see whales.

When we reach the mouth of the lagoon, we can see whales everywhere. We do not have our Italian friends to serenade them, but all six of us scan the waters, calling out our sightings using the hour-of-the-clock designation to indicate location. Again, I am afraid to hope for a close encounter, knowing how rare they are. As we motor around, watching, my hopes sink. It becomes apparent that our driver is not following the rules. He's far too pushy, moving the boat too close to the whales, pursuing them even after it's clear that they are choosing to swim away from us. Several times he sets us on an intercept course and motors directly over top of them. All of us are getting concerned, and then irritated, and soon we start telling him to stop, to back off, and to wait. Finally, he seems to get the message. Shortly afterwards, we approach a shallow area where a number of mother-baby pairs are lingering. It reminds me of human mothers taking their children to a park to play. We cruise slowly around and across the area, unapologetically ordering our driver to stop or slow down as we feel necessary. Apparently, it has worked: a mother-baby pair approaches us, nosing up to the boat. They are a bit more reserved than Mama and Baby Slash had been, usually staying just out of reach, but hovering near and under us. The mother surfaces first to check us out and then submerges, spending most of her time supporting her baby. At one point, she rolls over on her back cradling her baby beside her, using her right flipper to support it up next to the boat. The pair stay with us for about 20 minutes before deciding to move away from the shallow area.

We motor around for another 15 minutes or so before our driver nudges the throttle up and points us toward home. We have only been out for about two hours, but we had gotten a later start than scheduled and we still have a lot of miles to travel today once we reach land. It is a bit disappointing to end it so soon, but still, we have had another encounter, in spite of our driver, and just being out on the ocean, surrounded so closely by so many of these incredible creatures, is extraordinary and deeply satisfying. So I settle back to enjoy the return. It is very low tide by now and the salt marshes along the eastern shore are above the water line, yielding up their treasures to the hundreds of birds that stalk the flats. Unlike Guerrero Negro, there is no ESSA here with its vast acreage of salt ponds. These marshes and this lagoon remain virtually untouched by human industry. As the final destination of so many migratory species, the salt marshes provide a haven, sustenance, and breeding ground for the birds, just as the lagoon itself does for the whales.

When we reach Kuyima Camp, we climb out of the panga and walk barefoot across the sand flats toward the shore. I walk with my eyes downcast, scanning intently, hoping for treasures. The receding tide has revealed scattered patches of short bright green sea grass and the moist sand glistens in the sun, dotted with dozens of small snails. Looking closely at a shallow fist-sized depression in the sand, I'm excited to discover the round ruffled-edge collar of moon snail eggs. The same warm brown color as the sand, they only reveal themselves by that distinctive dent in the sand. We find about a half-dozen of them scattered across our path.

After picking our way carefully through the piles of rip-rap close to shore, we all gather in the palapa for a modest but tasty lunch of lentil soup, followed by a wonderfully succulent fresh white sea bass. Then, sadly, it is time to begin our long journey north.

As I gaze once more out my window, the boojums and cardons and elephant trees and ocotillos and creosote bushes surge majestically around me in great slow waves, floating on a sea of sand. As I look without, I also look within, seeing once more in my mind the flukes and flippers, the spy-hops and breaches, the gentle cradling of a baby by its mother, the crusty barnacles and soft pink sea lice on Mama's back, the pure white scar on Baby's side, and the soft receptive presence gazing back at me from that great dark eye. I feel once more the light wet spray of Baby's breath on my face; it is a whispered caress and a benediction.

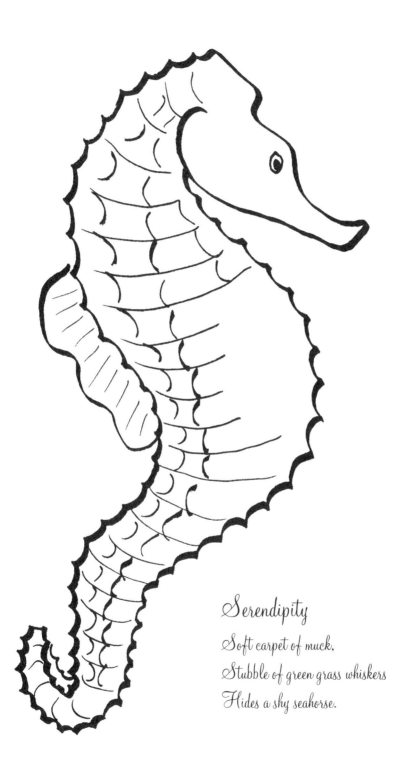

Serendipity

Soft carpet of muck,
Stubble of green grass whiskers
Hides a shy seahorse.

Diving Amok

*A*mok is a Malay word meaning "furious attack." In English, the word is spelled either amok or amuck and the American Heritage Dictionary gives two meanings: (1) in a frenzy to do violence or kill; and (2) in a blind, heedless manner. The phrase "to run amok" implies going crazy out of control over something. Given my recent experiences in the ocean waters off of Papua New Guinea, I would propose a third meaning: (3) going crazy over muck diving.

I had never heard of muck diving until the fall of 1999 when we began making plans for our vacation the following spring. We had chosen Papua New Guinea (otherwise and more fondly known as PNG) as our destination because of its reputation for having exceptionally beautiful, unspoiled reefs with some of the greatest biomass and biodiversity of any ocean area in the world. The woman who first told me about muck diving was an experienced diver who had been to PNG a number of times and was very enthusiastic about this particular variant of sport diving. She effectively communicated the strength of her enthusiasm but didn't provide me with any meaningful description of what muck is exactly. Consequently, I had visions of swimming through something akin to pea soup, groping along an unseen bottom by feel. Why in the world would anyone be so enthusiastic about that?

So it was with some trepidation, and more than a little skepticism, that Jon and I donned our dive gear and prepared to plunge into the waters of Bunama Beach, a small cove near the south end of Normanby Island. We reached the bottom at 16 feet and it was then that I understood for the first time what the word "muck" referred to: It was the bottom, not the water. The bottom of the cove was a large, flat, gently sloping expanse of gray silt and sand. In some areas this muck was practically featureless, but nearby we could see areas covered by a stubble of short green sea grass.

We set out toward the sea grass and found a small plastic bottle-float tied by a string to one of the blades of grass. This was the method that the boat crew used to mark items of particular interest so they would be easier for us to find. We finned our way over to the float and searched long and carefully for some item of interest. Finding none near the float, we turned our attention to a carpet anemone a couple of feet away. This particular anemone had quite a few of the Panda anemone fish and 3-spot dascyllus in residence—a great photo opportunity. My camera was rigged for doing close-up work so I carefully settled myself down on my stomach across the silt and began taking pictures while Jon assisted by occasionally herding errant fish back into the clutches of my framer.

We were thoroughly engrossed in our shooting, watching the larger female Pandas nip and bully their much smaller male companions while the dascyllus darted about, proclaiming that it wasn't their problem. I'd taken about a half-dozen shots when my concentration was infiltrated by a chuckle and someone tapped me on the leg. Turning my head, I discovered that there were three other divers near the float, all apparently searching the sea grass for that elusive whatever. Jon and I lifted ourselves up off the silt—carefully, so that we didn't disturb the bottom and kick up clouds of silt to turn the water to murk—and joined in the search. I quickly spotted the probable target: a dainty seahorse whose green coloring matched the grass to which he clung with his curled tail. I pointed excitedly and we all zeroed in on the little creature for a closer look. Fortunately, seahorses tend to stay put rather than running away, so we all had a chance to get up close and personal and to take as many photos as we wanted.

This was certainly an entertaining and enlightening beginning for our first muck dive! Jon and I continued across the muck, working our way toward a sunken jetty at the far end of the cove. Along the way, I spotted a beautiful, fluffy foot-tall sea pen sticking straight up from the muck but Jon didn't see it and, as he passed, his fins came too close to the bottom, kicking up a cloud of silt before I could close in for a photo. The jetty was a large jumble of broken concrete slabs populated by a variety of corals and small fish. Jon went to work with the wide-angle camera, chasing fish and maneuvering to frame the small coral heads. In the meantime,

I found several small brown pipefish slinking about. These delicate little animals look like seahorses that have lost their curl and they are in fact closely related to seahorses. I also saw a wonderful little long-horned cowfish and several black and white striped cardinal fish, but was unable to catch them with my camera.

Just off the jetty in the sand, we found a large group of inch-high sand hills. These volcano-shaped structures are formed by tube-worms which were too shy to show themselves to us, preferring to remain tucked safely in their burrows. Not too far from the tube-worm village, we had the opportunity to observe and photograph several burrows inhabited by sentinel gobies, each with its blind shrimp roommate. This is a fascinating example of mutually bene-ficial symbiosis; the goby stands watch just outside the burrow, alerting the shrimp to any danger, while the shrimp works con-stantly to keep the burrow well excavated and clear. We stopped at a distance from one of the burrows so we wouldn't alert the resident gobie and watched as the shrimp emerged frequently from their joint tenancy home, busily pushing piles of excess sand and silt out beyond the burrow's edge.

On the way back to the boat, we found a marvelous little fish unlike any we had ever seen before. It was a beautiful green mottled with white, which served to camouflage it very well among the sea grass. Only about four inches long, its almond-shaped body was accented with a large vertical spine at the front of its dorsal fin. It was remarkably docile for a fish, not quite cooperative, but at least placid while we maneuvered to photograph it.

Leaving the sea grass, we continued back across the naked muck, pausing for one final photo-op when we found a sunken log with a gorgeous lionfish nearby, its feathery brown and white striped fins fully extended as it levitated in the blue water. Lionfish are ideal subjects for the underwater photographer; not only are they exotically beautiful, but they are also extremely slow swimming and, hence, easy to photograph.

We finally ran out of film and reluctantly returned to the boat, very excited by our first experience with muck diving. In the shallow water, moving very slowly and carefully to avoid stirring up the silt, we had spent almost an hour and a half and I still hadn't used up all my air! We told the crew about our strange little green fish and were told that it is a Diamond Leatherjacket—fairly rare, and we were the first to see one on this trip.

On our next muck dive, which was a night dive, the highlight was finding a large Harp snail that was out stalking the muck for a meal. The mantle of this animal is much larger than its shell and spreads out on the bottom as the creature glides along. As I positioned the metal framer of my close-up camera in front of the animal, it actually reared up and lunged toward the framer as though to attack. The Harp snail is carnivorous, using its mantle to suffocate crabs for its meals. If some other creature attacks it, the snail can discard the large back portion of its mantle like a lizard discarding its tail.

On subsequent muck dives, we found many more strange and fascinating creatures: A school of razorfish, swimming in unison with their heads down, their bodies so narrow that they disappear if they rotate 90° from a flat side view; three tiny 6-inch-long black and white banded pipefish, their tails punctuated by flat little paddles with bull's-eye markings; a school of inch-long black fish with white racing stripes, hiding under a rotten log, swarming and writhing like a medusa-head of hyper-active snakes; a small turtle gliding past us into the shallows; a tiny transparent anemone shrimp, almost invisible on its home carpet anemone; a beautiful blue nudibranch, its racing stripes and feathery gills painted a brilliant chromium yellow; and a large, bright red hermit crab with white polka-dots, which actually seemed to pose cooperatively as I moved its shell slightly to get the right angle for a photo.

We spent hours in the water on these dives, enthralled by the marvelous creatures that inhabit the muck. Given a chance, I will most definitely go back and do it again: I've truly gone amok over muck diving!

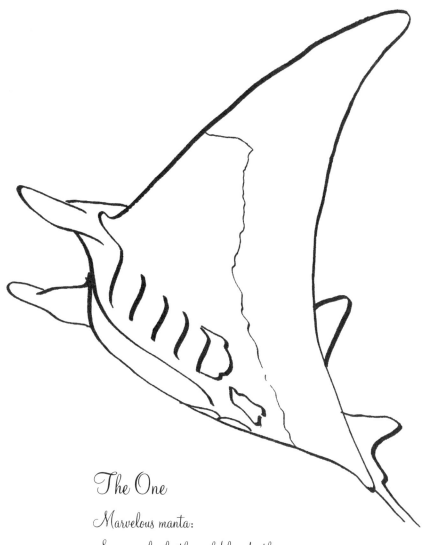

The One

Marvelous manta:
Soaring slowly through blue depths
We glide together.

El Bajo

*H*ow can I begin to describe the indescribable? How can I express in words an experience that is, ultimately, completely beyond words? A moment in time when time ceases, when self merges with other and becomes universe: The words reverberate in my head, smacking of pretense and artifice. But the experience was real, more intensely real than I could ever have dreamed. It has resonated in my memory for two decades now. Countless times I have thought about trying to write it down on paper. Several times I actually tried, without success. So now I try once more....

It is August of 1979. Jon and I are on a week-long diving trip in the Sea of Cortez, living with 20 of our friends on board the *Mar-Isla*, a 120-foot converted buoy-tender out of La Paz in Baja, California. The trip is our 5th anniversary present to ourselves and it has been wonderful so far, with perfect weather, gorgeous sunrises and sunsets, excellent diving, and the camaraderie of good friends. The crew wait on us hand and foot, helping us with our dive gear, cleaning the fish that we spear and ensuring that we have comfortable quarters, plenty of food, and as much air in our tanks as we can consume. The skipper grumbles good naturedly about how much diving we do. He and the crew are not used to entertaining divers who want to do a warm-up dive before breakfast, three dives before lunch, three dives before dinner, and a final dive after dinner.

On this particular morning, the excitement on board is a crackling current that flashes from diver to diver, infecting the crew, and even reflected in the modulating hum of the boat's engines. We are at El Bajo, The Sea Mount, an underwater mountain, the top of which lies about 60 feet below the surface. The mount harbors a wealth of life: corals, sponges, algaes, and countless schools of fish.

It also has hammerheads. A hammerhead shark is a preposterous looking beast, with a head that must have been designed by the imaginative young techno-artists at Industrial Light and Magic; its eyes attach at the very end of a snout that has been transmogrified into a pair of long, flat protuberances. Those protuberances are absurd enough, but it is the front edge of the snout that necessitates the word preposterous. This leading edge is scalloped, adding a feminine and somewhat frivolous accent to the animal's visage. One expects to see such a head in a Space Bar somewhere on the other side of Aldebaran. Not here. Not now. And certainly not attached to a long, large, sleek, torpedo-shaped body with a lethal-looking scythe for a tail.

We had heard that in this place the hammerheads swim in schools and we just confirmed it with our own eyes. On our first dive here we descended to the top of the Mount and then continued down its side, leisurely exploring the seascape and its inhabitants. As I looked up from the reef structure to enjoy the expanse of mountainside that was visible in the clear tropical water, I detected movement out at the very edge of visibility. As I focused, the movement became clear: A pattern of dark blue shapes streaming slowly and sinuously from right to left across my field of view. The vision ripped through my eyes and exploded in my mind: hammerheads!

An entire wall of them, evenly spaced, swimming in unison, like some animated wallpaper in a vast blue room of dreams. I was stunned, terrified, fascinated. I looked around to find Jon; he was close behind with the camera. I made a calling noise with my vocal chords to get his attention and pointed toward the "wallpaper." He nodded in reply and swam toward me. But he didn't stop. He raised the camera and increased his speed. As my eyes followed around and re-focused on the moving wall of sharks, I saw that one of them had broken from the school and was swimming directly toward us. And Jon was swimming directly toward it. *NO!* I shouted in my mind. *Don't DO that! Come BACK!* But I knew that he had to get close, he had to get a shot of that shark.

I reached down and grabbed a large rock, giving it a bear-hug, attempting to become part of the reef as I throat-shouted after my loving, charming, insane husband. The shark was close enough now that I could get some sense of its size—about eight feet, I'd say —big enough to do some damage if it chose. I watched in horror as the gap between Jon and the beast narrowed. Light flashed suddenly as Jon triggered the camera with its attached strobe. Instantly, the shark veered to the left and swam rapidly off into the deep to join its cohorts. I stopped doing my rock-imitation and quickly scanned the full area that was visible around us, seeing no sign of any sharks. When I got close enough to Jon I shook my fist at him in a feeble attempt to communicate, "I love you, you stupid idiot—you could have been killed—don't ever scare me like that again." Then our eyes met and the electric excitement bridged the gap between us and we laughed together silently, behind our face plates.

We've been back on board the boat for about an hour now so we are past the initial trembling of knees and shaking of bodies that seized us on our return—the emotional aftermath of our encounter with the sharks. We have told and re-told our adventure to our friends and we are ready now for another dive. The thrill of antic-ipating another shark encounter is excitement enough, but now an even greater thrill of anticipation grips us. We have spotted several manta rays nearby, the tips of their wings flipping daintily out of the water, much as humans dangle their fingers in the water. From this distance it is hard to tell how big they are: the giant Pacific manta rays can have a 10–20-foot wingspan.

We watch intently to get a better glimpse of them, chattering among ourselves, pointing and whooping when we observe move-ment or spot another manta. We talk about their size, about whether or not they are dangerous maneaters. No, someone says, they are harmless filter-feeders, munching on nothing larger than tiny plankton and krill, which they scoop into their mouths using large leathery flaps on either side of their head. We've seen their smaller cousins, the bat-rays, many times on our dives around California's Channel Islands. Bat-rays have the unfortunate charac-teristic that, when they are dead (usually killed) and dried, their bodies form a grotesque devil-like face. Hence the Mexicans call them Devil Fish and run a brisk business selling these pathetic little corpses to the Americans who frequent the shops in Tijuana, Ensenada, and other border tourist towns.

We have never seen manta rays before and the prospect of meeting them on a dive compels us to hasten our pre-dive ritual. My hands are trembling as I pull on my tights and leotard over my swimsuit. The water is wonderfully warm—about 80°F—so there is no need for a wet-suit, but the dangers of corals and other stinging animals make it advisable to wear a protective skin. I strap my diving knife to my leg, push my head through my buoyancy control vest, heft my weight belt around my waist, hook my game-bag to the belt, and take inventory to make sure that I have both fins, both gloves, and my mask with snorkel. By now, a crewmember has picked up my tank and holds it as I slip into it. Having such assistance is a vacation luxury and it makes me feel like a princess at the ball, slipping into her fur wrap for a carriage ride around the estate. I giggle nervously at the incongruity of the image and check to see if Jon is ready. We walk heavily and awkwardly over to the side of the boat, carefully put our fins on as the deck sways and pitches under us, adjust our masks, put on our gloves, put our life-giving regulators in our mouths, draw a test breath to ensure that our air is flowing freely, take a sighting in the direction we want to head, and fall.

The blue water that engulfs us deepens and intensifies in color as we descend toward El Bajo. We are about 100 yards off of the main pinnacle, sinking down to a relatively flat reef area at about 90 feet. When we reach the bottom, we stop to check our depth gauges and adjust our vests to neutral buoyancy. As Jon checks out the camera and locks the strobe arm into place, I scan the area and choose a direction to explore. I point. Jon nods in agreement. We kick slowly and leisurely off across the reef. I allow my eyes and mind to open, to expand my awareness so that I can connect with as much of my surroundings as possible. I want to explore it all, from the great expanses of reef vistas down to the tiniest details of individual coral polyps, nudibranchs, and the myriad of other creatures that dwell there.

We move weightlessly, without effort, in slow motion through paradise. I stop swimming for a moment, righting myself to 'stand' a foot or so above the reef and look back at Jon.

I can hardly believe my eyes; as though in a dream I see a large manta ray close behind him, the graceful movement of its wings carrying it past him close enough that he reaches out and up and gently touches the very tip of its wing. I see that it does not flinch from the contact. The manta is now moving directly toward me and as it soars over my head I give a single kick of my fins and reach out. My gloved hand connects with the base of the animal's left wing on the trailing edge, close to its body. Its skin is soft and leathery with a sandpaper finish that makes it easy to keep my grip. The manta is not startled but rather seems as though it has been expecting me. I feel it exert a surge of extra power that flows from its compact body out through the expanse of its wings, 'digging in' to adjust its stroke for the additional weight it now carries.

We glide across the reef. Time ceases. The beast and I are a single entity, connected and in harmony. There is no universe—only the rhythmic motion. Our wings rise and fall, rise and fall endlessly, and we are engulfed in the deep blue. My eyes are riveted to those huge wings, black above and creamy white below. We are nothing more than the power and poetry of those wings.

Reluctantly, slowly, I pull my mind back into myself and begin to think about where I am. I have no concept of how much time has passed or what my depth is or where I am. I look around and see Jon up ahead. I realize that we must have circled the reef and are now returning to our starting point. As we soar past Jon I look at him intently, feeling like a kid, demanding with my thoughts that he take a picture. He takes several and then I release my hold and drop back into the mundane world. The other part of my being soars off into the distance and is soon lost from sight. I am filled simultaneously with a sense of incredible fullness and enormous loss. I know that what I have just experienced has changed me deeply and permanently. A fragment of a quote from a long-forgotten source resonates in my mind:

> When windows open,
> when doors beckon,
> When once you have experienced something,
> You can never,
> permanently,
> say no to it.

As I write this now, 20 years later, I still carry with me in my heart the soul of that magnificent beast. And my soul still soars on great black wings of grace and power and beauty in a timeless blue void.

Extreme

AUGUST 20, 2000

I'm envious, really. And angry with myself for feeling so inadequate. If they can do it, then I should be able to do it too. I've tried very hard to dismiss the Eco-Challenge as just another macho publicity stunt, but I was there in Sabah eight years ago and I envy her—I envy all of them—for being there now. The Eco-Challenge is Extreme Adventure, pitting 4-person teams not only against each other, but also against some of the most rugged and challenging conditions that Nature can provide. Seventy-six teams are competing this year: 304 people from all over the world. For 12 days these teams will race against each other over a 320-mile course through the jungles, rivers, oceans, and mountains of northeastern Borneo. Each team must be self-sufficient and self-sustaining, moving under their own power, and they must complete the race together.

"She"—the object of my envy—is Maureen, a colleague of mine and a member of the team sponsored by my employer. Maureen's teammates include two other members of our company, plus Maureen's brother Bill who is the team captain. I worry about how the team will function in the remote, primitive, and demanding environment of Borneo, particularly under the extreme conditions of the Eco-Challenge race. I fear for their health and safety. I envy their courage and commitment to adventure. And I feel so inadequate, knowing that I would not dream of attempting such a race.

My cowardice arises from the fact that I have Addison's disease, a condition in which a person's immune system destroys their adrenal glands. Without treatment, the condition is fatal. It is incurable, but with treatment most individuals can lead a reasonably normal life, as long as they avoid highly stressful situations. Although the condition is very rare, I know it intimately, having

159

lived with it for 25 years. Under normal conditions, the treatment for Addison's disease is pretty simple: small doses of cortisone are taken every day to replace what should be produced by the adrenal glands. A mere 30 mg per day is all that is required to keep an Addisonian alive and functional—under normal conditions. Under conditions such as the teams will be experiencing in Borneo, it would take probably three or more times that amount. The exact amount needed is highly variable from individual to individual, and from situation to situation, determined only by feel and guesswork. Too risky for me. So, I am merely a remote spectator, observing the race voyeuristically by logging on to the official Eco-Challenge website from the comfort and safety of my home computer.

AUGUST 21, 2000 (DAY 1)

The race started today. I just watched a video online showing the scene at the Dragon Inn in Semporna as the teams readied their outriggers, called perahus, and set off on the first leg of the race, paddling/sailing from Semporna to Sanbakat and from there to Boyhaydulong, two small islands off the coast. Yesterday, I was apprehensive, with very mixed emotions. Today as I watched the video, I got caught up in the excitement as the adventure began.

I remember so well our own overnight stay at the Dragon Inn, barely able to sleep for the anticipation of the next day, when we would journey by boat to Sipadan. Our plan had been to spend a week diving on that tiny, remote island. The Dragon Inn is a charming wooden single-story structure that rambles on stilts out over the bay. Each room has a private bath which is actually a door-less glorified outhouse on the narrow porch behind the room. A modern porcelain toilet empties its contents straight down through the floor into the bay. I realize that this is the last vestige of civilization that Bill and Maureen and their teammates will experience for the next 12 days.

AUGUST 22, 2000 (DAY 2)

My heart was in my throat as I scrolled down through the list of team rankings on the webpage for the second time. I hadn't seen my team on the list. What was wrong? Then I realized that I had viewed only the first page of the rankings. Clicking rapidly to the second page, I found them; their ranking is 52. I sighed in relief—they are safe and they are still in the race. Each team must split today, with two members continuing to paddle in their perahu while the other two follow a separate course that involves swimming, coasteering, hiking, and snorkeling before meeting up again with their teammates at Passport Control (PC) checkpoint 7 on the island of Tetagon. The paddlers are expected to spend about 2 or 3 hours getting to the rendezvous. The other half of the team may take 8 to 12 hours to cover their part of the course.

Mark Burnett, the originator, organizer, and motivating force behind the Eco-Challenge, has issued a warning to the teams that a storm is coming with high winds, heavy rains, and waves up to 6 feet high. Some teams push on in their perahus—in the dark of the night—in spite of the warning. Others decide to wait it out. I don't know what decision my team has made.

I remember the storms. Even though Sabah is called "The Land Beneath the Wind," meaning that it does not get the frightful typhoons that always seem to pass further north, it does get frequent storms. During our week on Sipadan, we had at least one storm every night. Our little thatched-roof hut had shuddered and danced on its stilts and the darkness was punctuated by lightening which flashed and crashed and rumbled at unpredictable intervals. One night, a large fireball of lightening exploded just above the trees directly behind our camp, a mere 30 yards or so from our hut. The explosion was the loudest noise I have ever heard—a scream of terror tore through my throat and my body reflexively tightened into the fetal position. I lay curled up for a long time until my breathing and pulse settled back to normal. The storm continued to rage until first light.

I wish my team a safe journey through the storm.

AUGUST 23, 2000 (DAY 3)

Three teams have been disqualified during the sailing leg; one team had its perahu break into several pieces and sink, though all four members were rescued and unharmed. The teams are arriving now at PC 12 which is located at Silam on the coast of Borneo. There is a full camp there with showers and a medical staff. I've discovered that it is possible to send messages to the teams via the website so

I sent one to my team. I wished them good luck as they begin the mountain biking portion of the course and told them to enjoy the beauty of Borneo along with the challenge.

The first serious injury has occurred; the captain of one of the teams fell off his bike while trying to negotiate a sharp turn on the muddy path. He fell onto a branch which punctured his chest and collapsed one of his lungs. He was rescued quickly, treated in the field, and then airlifted to a hospital in Kota Kinabalu. The reports state that he is now resting comfortably.

A new kind of teamwork has emerged. Eight of the 2-person teams got lost on one of the islands during the perahu portion of the race. The eight teams banded together, sharing water and food and cooperating in a methodical exploration to find the trail. In another instance, one woman injured her leg badly and could not walk. Members of two other teams carried her to safety, disregarding the fact that this would delay their progress.

I scan every press release for news of my team. So far, they are apparently continuing without incident. Their ranking is now 51—they have moved up one position.

AUGUST 24, 2000 (DAY 4)

It took the best teams 8–9 hours to complete the mountain-bike leg of the race, traveling through the jungle, across rivers, and up and down the rugged terrain. Once they reached PC 14, the Danim Valley Field Center, they traded in their bikes for their jungle trekking gear and began the arduous hike on foot through the rain forest. The slower teams are still working to complete the mountain bike segment. There are now 68 teams still officially in the competition, though some of the teams that have been disqualified have elected to continue the race unranked. My team has moved up to the 45th rank now and I sit at my computer half a world away and cheer them on.

I remember the rain forests of Borneo: the intense heat, the close, humid air, the trees soaring 150 feet upward, the darkness under the canopy, the endless cacophony of birds and insects, the chatter and shrieks of the tribes of monkeys. A place of exotic living beauty, the Sabah rain forest is among the tallest and oldest in the world. A member of one of the disqualified teams said,

"We came here as much to see the country as to race. We're not going home without doing that." My colleague Maureen put a message on the website: "*This is the adventure of a lifetime!*"

How I wish I were there.

AUGUST 25, 2000 (DAY 5)

The leading teams are completing the rain forest trek now, returning to the Danim Valley Research Center, at the same time that the stragglers are arriving from the biking segment. Today is the cutoff point for staying in the race. My team barely made it—they are ranked 54th now, the last officially ranked team. Another 18 teams are continuing unranked.

Today's photo galley on the webpage includes a picture of my team. Bill sits on the ground in the back, leaning against the wall of a building and the other two men are leaning back on a wooden gear crate. Nearby, one of their bikes, completely encrusted in mud, is propped against two red oil barrels. Maureen sits in the right lower corner of the photo, her back to the camera, so I cannot see her face. Several Coke bottles and cans of Pringles are scattered on the ground near their bare feet. Unlike their team photo taken before the race, none of them are smiling now. They all look strained and weary, but determined.

Another photo in today's gallery shows a narrow wood and cable suspension bridge, a hint of what lies in store for the rain forest trek. I remember crossing such bridges, hanging on tightly and stepping awkwardly as the bridge jerked and heaved in unexpected ways beneath my feet. Every time I have crossed one of them I cannot help but laugh uncontrollably, feeling as giddy as a drunkard on a sidewalk.

I've just printed off 16 pages of messages that have been left on the website for my team. They are from friends, relatives, and colleagues; some of the messages are funny:

> *From: Dad*
> Kevin—*please do not lose to the bunnies (the Playboy Extreme team).*

However, most are full of encouragement and pride:

"Hey you guys! We're so proud of you and what you're doing—can't imagine what it must be like. Best wishes for a safe and speedy journey."

And a few show concern and worry:

"Where are you guys ... You've been gone 19 hours from PC 14 and the slowest time to 15 so far is 18:02 ... Something has got to be up ... Hope you get back in the game."

Lisa, Bill's wife, has sent many messages, all of them full of love and caution:

"We hope you are doing OK and are in good spirits ... Make sure you are eating to stay strong! ... We miss you and love you. Be safe and sensible."

The website now indicates that the team arrived at PC 14 after 18 hours and 42 minutes and are now on their way to PC 15. "Be safe and sensible," Lisa had said. Perhaps that is why it took them so long. Perhaps they stopped to rest and eat and rehydrate themselves. Dehydration can occur so easily in the rain forest, in spite of all the humidity. And the signs can be so subtle that you may not realize at first how parched you are until the condition is extreme.

The potential for dehydration, and its consequences, are significantly worse for an Addisonian than for a normal person. The adrenal glands produce aldosterone, which regulates the body's electrolytes and fluid balance. Without aldosterone a person rapidly becomes dehydrated even under normal conditions and can collapse as their body loses salt and their blood pressure plummets. I remember how surprised I was when I became dehydrated there. I wasn't doing anything strenuous—just riding on the tour bus, walking short distances through the jungle, strolling through a Buddhist temple, and sitting in a small boat as we motored up the river. I didn't realize that in spite of the humidity, the heat was rapidly sucking the water from my body. Weakness welled up like a huge wave, engulfing every muscle in my body. My heart began beating in a crazy, irregular pattern. I was dizzy and a tunnel of darkness began closing in on me.

I was fortunate that I was able to identify the cause before I reached the blackout point and doubly fortunate that there was a small store nearby where I was able to buy a large bottle of water. I didn't have any Florinef with me on that trip. Florinef is a synthetic aldosterone, which many Addisonians take regularly. Under normal conditions, I don't need it. In Borneo, it would have been very helpful. To compensate, I began carrying a large water bottle with me at all times and I smothered my food with salt at every meal.

AUGUST 26, 2000 (DAY 6)

My team has apparently been moving rapidly over the past 24 hours. They are now ranked 42nd—a great leap upward from yesterday's 54th rank. According to the website, they left PC 18 almost five hours ago. Being somewhat slow is lucky in this case: Mark Burnett decided late yesterday to cut out PC 19 because it included a long swim in a river that has become very swollen and treacherous due to torrential rains since the leading teams passed through. All the later teams including mine will be permitted to go directly to PC 20 from PC 18, although their times will be adjusted due to the course change.

In the meantime the leading team, Salomon Eco-Internet from the U.S., has passed PC 29. Looking at the map of the course I see that they have only three more segments to travel, mostly sailing in their perahu with a little scuba diving along the way, and they will be at PC 32—the finish of the race. Three other teams are in hot pursuit: France's Team Spie, Australia's Team Aussie Spirit, and New Zealand's Team Fairydown Fleet Cookie Time. The members of all of these teams are very experienced adventure racers, having competed in and in some cases won previous Eco-Challenges and other similar adventure races. The female member of the Salomon team is Robyn Benincasa, a resident of Del Mar, CA—the same community I live in. I wish I knew her!

Why do people risk their lives to endure the horrendous conditions and stresses of adventure races such as these? The usual answers of fame and fortune do not seem to be significant here. First place brings a purse of $50,000, which is substantially short of the estimated $55,000 in expenses that is required to field a 4-person team for such a race. As for fame, that seems to be in short supply also.

Other than the daily coverage provided on three Internet websites, I have seen no mention of the race in local newspapers or on TV. One website indicates that USA Network will air a TV program about the race next April.

The team biographies reveal a number of different motivations. Some have come seeking adventure and a chance to experience an exotic and foreign land. Many are inveterate competitors, spurred by the thrill and challenge of pitting their all against others. Some, like the former Playboy playmates of Team Playboy Extreme, want to prove to others that women can be more—much more—than merely soft and beautiful sexual objects. Some are seeking the limits of their own capabilities, competing as it were against themselves to find their own personal best.

All of these reasons resonate in my mind. My present envy and frustration have their roots in my own desire to experience adventure in far-flung locales. Competition? I remember with great clarity the exuberant joy I felt as a child, feeling the wind in my hair as I raced flat-out across the playground to beat my classmates. For the first time in my life, I feel a bond of sisterhood with those extraordinary Playmates. No longer do I see them as a reproach for my lack of perfect beauty—now I see them as sisters in my life-long battle to be seen as competent and to be taken seriously in spite of my gender.

As for personal best—ah, there's the heart of it for me. Over the years as my body has been insulted first by destruction of my adrenals and then in turn by destruction of my thyroid glands, and then my ovaries, and now my salivary glands, my energy level has gradually decreased and I have been forced to turn inward. I know that I cannot compete against others anymore—now I must compete with myself, seeking my own limits and the triumphs that come from within.

AUGUST 27, 2000 (DAY 7)

In a sense, the race is over now. The first three teams have completed the course: Team Salomon Eco-Internet is first, Team Spie is second, and Team Aussie Spirit is third. Seeing strong women such as Salomon's Robyn Benincasa and Aussie Spirit's Jane Hall compete and win is thrilling and fills me with pride and joy.

The winning team took just under 144 hours to complete the 306-mile course. In that 6 days' time, they slept for less than 12 hours total, with their longest rest being 2 hours.

But the most important part of the race yet remains; 45 other teams are still officially competing, along with an additional 18 teams that are continuing the course even though they have been officially disqualified. My team is still among the 48 official competitors and is now ranked at 33—another leap upward from yesterday's 42nd rank. Still, if one combines the official with the unofficial teams, my team is only in 46th place and is currently canoeing down the river somewhere between PC 21 and PC 22. The unranked Team Playboy Extreme would be ranked 16th if they were still officially in the race. They have completed the river canoeing segment and are now sailing down the coast toward PC 24.

On a prominent corner at the entry into my neighborhood stands a very large tree. I have walked past that tree almost every morning for the 10 years I have lived here and it has inspired and warmed me with its size and strength and beauty. Ever since my return from Borneo, this tree has been my constant reminder of the rivers there. I remember on our long day's journey up river from Sandakan, there was one tree, much larger than all the rest, which stood at a bend in the river, dominating the forest, its soaring reflection reaching out to us across the muddy water. The villagers living along the river called it a Spirit Tree and believed that the souls of their ancestors lived there. As we glided past it on our way back down the river, the setting sun glowed from behind its great spreading canopy and I was touched by the soul of that magnificent tree.

The tree in my neighborhood is dying now, the leaves on half its branches already shriveled and dead, the remaining half beginning to wither and turn brown. It is the victim of our civilization's compulsion to have straight and level sidewalks; a year ago the street engineers amputated the largest root of the tree—the one that had lifted the sidewalk into an unruly up-and-down angle.

A new story on the website indicates that Team Fairydown Fleet Cookie Time, the reigning champion of the Eco-Challenge, has been forced to abandon the race. Their captain, John Howard, considered to be one of the best adventure racers ever, was brought to the field hospital with feet so badly damaged and sore that he was no longer able to walk. Although no other injuries have occurred that are as severe as the punctured chest and collapsed lung of Day 3, the reports indicate that there have been many injuries and illnesses along the way. One woman sustained a neck injury that "could have resulted in permanent paralysis," and one man sustained a "closed-head injury," which I assume to be a concussion. The extreme heat and humidity have made dehydration and heat exhaustion common. Other afflictions include lacerations, abrasions, blisters, leech bites, ulcers, fungal infections, and a foot condition called "trench foot," caused by days of immersion in rivers and ocean water.

Extreme. The word pops up over and over again, festering in my mind like an infected wound. It's a very popular concept in sports these days. Webster's dictionary defines extreme as: (1) at the end, farthest away, most remote; (2) last, final; (3) going to great lengths, excessive; and (4) very severe, drastic. Certainly those descriptions fit the Eco-Challenge race. What is the opposite of extreme? In mathematics, extreme means the first or last term of a series, as opposed to the mean. In college my friends and I jokingly referred to the "Mediocre Middle," a term of derision meant to dismiss the dull and the conventional. The Latin root of extreme is *extremus*, which is the superlative of exter, so the progression is exter, exterus, extremus: out, outer, outermost. The opposite of exter is inter, from the comparative form of which we get our word "interior." But Webster's does not say what the superlative form of inter is. Would it be inter, interus, intremus? Strange that we have the opposites exterior and interior, extrovert and introvert, but yet there is no intreme to oppose extreme.

AUGUST 28, 2000 (DAY 8)

The fatigue is always worse after a good night's sleep. I wake up with a pall of lassitude permeating my body and mind. A normal person's adrenal glands begin to produce a large amount of cortisone several hours before dawn, so that they awaken alert and ready to start the day. The longer I sleep, the lower my cortisone level drops. When my alarm goes off I stumble through the mental fog to find my morning dose of cortisone. After gulping it down with some water, I make a cup of tea and sit down at my computer to see how the race is going.

There is not much information available this morning. Ten teams have now finished the course. The latest update bulletin on the QuokkaSports site says "Relentless night-time storm. Heavy rain. Several teams in perahus...Others being held at PC 23." Although it is early morning for me, it is approaching midnight in Sabah. My team has completed the river canoeing segment and is one of the teams being held at PC 23. Their ranking is now 30th, up from 33 yesterday. Hopefully, the rain will give them a chance to get some much-needed rest.

One of Lisa's messages to Bill indicates that she had spoken with him by phone and she says, in part, "*...Stay strong and healthy ... I hope your injury is OK...*" At PC 18, having completed most of the jungle trek, the team posted several messages on the web. Maureen says, "*It has been a tough few days trekking and mountain biking through the jungle in foot deep mud...We WILL finish this race! PS— I HATE LEECHES!*" And Bill writes, "*Lisa and Eva, Having a great time. Miss you both terribly. With love.*"

I'm relieved that apparently Bill's injury is a fairly minor one. Being injured is the thing I fear most about traveling to remote locations like Borneo. For an Addisonian, even a moderately serious injury such as a broken leg can precipitate an Addisonian crisis, in which blood pressure and blood sugar levels drop rapidly, throwing the individual into extreme shock and then a coma. Without timely treatment of very large doses of cortisone and fluids, the person can die. It is a very scary business.

AUGUST 29, 2000 (DAY 9)

As of this morning, 14 teams have completed the race course. My team is ranked 30th still and has left PC 25. That means they are somewhere in the middle of the Madai Caves segment. After entering the huge limestone caves, each team must climb up vertical rattan ladders, jumar 150 feet up fixed ropes, cross a deep gorge on a rope (this is called a Tyrolean traverse), and then rappel 600 feet back down to the base of the caves. They will then sail their perahu back out to the islands they had visited early in the race, do a little scuba diving along the way, and finally sail back to Semporna to complete the race.

I've never seen the Madai Caves but we did visit the Batu Caves just north of Kuala Lumpur. There, the huge limestone caverns have been transformed into a Hindu shrine, which can only be reached by climbing 272 steps. In situations such as this, I always make sure that I take an extra dose or two of my cortisone to compensate for the increased physical stress. We browsed the shops at the base of the shrine to allow enough time for the cortisone to enter my blood stream and then we started up the long stairway. We climbed slowly in the intense heat, stopping several times to rest and watch the antics of the long-tailed macaques that roamed freely everywhere. By the time we reached the caves at the top, we were drenched with sweat and more than ready to rest in the cool shadows of the shrines. There are no shrines in the Madai Caves, only bats and bird's nests and thick layers of black, slippery guano. There will be no rest for my team in the Madai Caves either. They must keep pushing onward, back to the coast to complete the final segments of the race.

In the meantime, Team Playboy Extreme has already reclaimed their perahu and sailed to PC 30. From there they will continue out to a small island for a brief scuba dive before finally sailing back to Semporna. They continue to be the brunt of many jokes and derogatory comments and yet, like that other bunny, they just keep going and going and going. Although they are listed with the unranked teams as being in 48th place, their actual time and position gives them a ranking of 17. An extraordinary accomplishment for a bunch of blonde bimbo bunnies!

AUGUST 30, 2000 (DAY 10)

The Bunnies have finished at the top of the list of 9 disqualified teams that actually finished the race. Their final time would have put them in 21st place had they not been disqualified. Their skill and courage and determination fill me with pleasure and pride.

The photo gallery for today includes a photo of my team. They are standing together in white shirts and climbing gear, strong and relaxed and smiling. Bill has his arm around Maureen. Behind them looms the sheer limestone cliff of the Madai Caves, wrapped all around in the bright living green of the rain forest. A beautiful and heart-warming photo.

Today's status report indicates that they have completed the scuba diving at PC 31 and are on their way back to Semporna.

PC 31 is a tiny island called Pulau Sibuan, which is frosted all around with white sand beaches and crowned with palm trees. The report says that a walk from one end to the other and back again takes 20 minutes. That means it is even smaller than Sipadan, which took us about 40 minutes to walk around. The rules of the race state that each team must spend 90 minutes on the island, regardless of how long it takes them to do their 30-foot dive. That way they have a chance to relax a little and enjoy a taste of paradise.

I find it a bit strange that diving is included in the race. Diving is essentially a solitary and non-competitive sport. Even when one dives with a buddy, communication is pretty much limited to a couple of very basic hand gestures and the occasional wink of an eye or holding of gloved hands if your buddy is also your mate. Divers don't compete to dive deeper or swim further; competition is an optional overlay, another sport that may be combined with the diving, such as spear-fishing or photography contests. Or Eco-Challenges.

Of course, it would be criminal to be in Borneo and not experience the ocean reefs there and so every team must spend their 90 minutes at PC 31, non-competitively enjoying the beautiful coral reefs with their throngs of fishes and lovely turquoise waters. I remember the hours we spent diving the waters of Sipadan, drifting as the currents carried us along the coral walls. Turtles sailed past us in majestic slow motion and even the sharks seemed to be relaxing, swimming slowly and languidly into the current. I remember drifting into the middle of three large schools of small reef fishes. They surrounded me in swirling, dizzying walls of flashing color. I was completely engulfed in the magic of the ocean. I hope the magic touches my team at Pulau Sibuan.

AUGUST 31, 2000 (DAY 11)

My team finished just after noon today and I am elated over their success. They were the 37th team to finish, but their official rank was 29th, due to the fact that some teams are unranked. In an article on the QuokkaSports site, Mark Burnett is quoted as saying,

> *"All of my projects…have to do with human beings in stressful situations working in groups to overcome adversity…*

All expeditions in history have succeeded or failed based upon the human dynamics, and not upon physicality."

Certainly the human dynamics have been a major factor in this race and all of the 53 teams that have finished the course have succeeded in working together to overcome tremendous challenges.

But just as certainly, the race has demanded a great deal of physicality of all participants. I am in awe of them. I know I do not have nearly the strength or endurance they have and I would be unable to complete such a race. Perhaps I would have been able to do so 15 years ago, when I was Maureen's age and had only Addison's disease to contend with, but I will never know.

Nevertheless, I have had many adventures of my own over the years and I look forward to many more in the years to come. My mind goes back to our last evening on Sipadan. After dinner, Jon and I went out on the pier. We sat in silence watching the stars reflected on the surface of the water, and then we realized that the lights were moving. They were "flashlight fish"—a school of small fish that have luminescent eye-patches with eyelids that blink to create the flashing effect. It was as though 30 or 40 huge stars had fallen into the ocean at our feet and were playing a game of hide and seek with each other. As though outer space, the extreme limits of the universe, had collapsed into inner space, the depths of the ocean. And there it is that I always return: for "intreme" adventure, in the innermost places of the ocean and my heart.

> *To see the universe in a grain of sand*
> *And heaven in a wildflower*
> *Hold infinity in the palm of your hand*
> *And eternity in an hour.*
> — William Blake

Awakening

My rush-hour trance:
But the bright and silver sea
Dances me alive.

To Live Before the Wind

*"They are the lads that always live before the wind.
They are accounted a lucky omen. If you yourself can
withstand three cheers at beholding these vivacious fish,
then heaven help ye; the spirit of godly gamesomeness is
not in ye."*

— Herman Melville

The scene is heart-rending, full of suspense and pathos. The young boy, Jesse, stands out on the breakwater, tears streaming down his face as he urges Willy, the only friend he has ever known, to make a run for it, while the cops and Willy's owner race to recapture the great killer whale. After endless minutes of hesitation, Willy gathers himself and makes an astonishing slow-motion leap over the forbidding wall of rocks, over Jesse's head, and rushes off to join the waiting pod of whales. As the closing credits roll, we see Willy loping, leaping, and playing with his long-lost family in the brilliant blue waters of freedom and we know that his evil owners, whose sole motive for wanting to keep the whale was to make a big profit, will never be able to recapture him.

Ah, life is so simple and clean in Hollywood. The storyline of *Free Willy* is as black and white as its hero. I know full well that life isn't like that and yet I am as susceptible as thousands of others to the theme of connecting—truly communicating—with an animal of such obvious beauty and power and intelligence, and to the struggles of both boy and whale to regain freedom and family. Thus, I was not surprised to discover that so many people around the world were supporting the real-life campaign to return Keiko, the whale that played Willy in the film, to the wild. Many people disapprove deeply of keeping such obviously intelligent mammals in captivity,

175

and are highly critical of organizations such as Sea World for opportunistically exploiting them for entertainment and profit. Certainly such crass exploitation has occurred, sometimes with pathetic and tragic consequences. On the other hand, Sea World and other organizations like it claim that their profits serve to fund serious research and that the entertainment also serves to educate the public. What then is the reality?

When I discovered that Sea World offers a program called Trainer for a Day, I leaped at the opportunity to have my own first-hand experience with whales and dolphins, to see for myself what life was like for marine mammals living their lives in captivity.

The dolphin muscled her way past her three companions and lifted her grinning head out of the water at my feet, squealing and squeaking excitedly at us. Without hesitation I began mimicking the sounds and for a few moments the two of us chatted happily together. She tried some rapid clicks, which I failed miserably at imitating, but I think I was pretty good at the squeals and squeaks. Never mind that I had no idea what the sounds might mean. Never mind that the scene might appear more than a bit ridiculous to an "objective" by-stander. I felt an instant and strong connection with this exuberant, sleek gray mammal, and at that moment, nothing else in the world mattered. Her name was Malibu. As we talked with Wendy, our trainer and guide for the day, I discovered that Malibu had been one of the baby dolphins that I had seen during the Dolphin Show on a visit to Sea World two or three years previously. I had been charmed by her then, watching her tiny form as she roamed the pool freely, attempting to imitate the tricks that the well-trained adult dolphins were performing. Now she was nearly a full grown adult, a Pacific Bottlenose dolphin weighing in at about 400 pounds, and herself a well-trained member of the Dolphin Show ensemble.

Malibu's three companions were Beaker, Misty, and Bullet. Beaker was named for her distinctive overbite, a rarity among bottlenose dolphins, which typically have their lower jaws jutting out past their uppers. Misty was a lovely soft gray with beautiful facial markings. Bullet, like her name, was small and dark and very sleek, with a much more pointed nose, or rostrum, than her compatriots. Wendy explained that Bullet was a hybrid, a cross between a Pacific Bottlenose and a smaller species, the Common Dolphin. Her creation had been an accident, because the Sea World trainers would not deliberately interbreed different species. There was one other mixed-breed dolphin like Bullet that we would meet later, a rescued animal named Bella. Both were exceptionally bright, generally learning more quickly than either of their parent species—perhaps an example of "hybrid vigor."

The four dolphins bobbed and jostled together in the training pool as Wendy explained our schedule for the day. As a birthday present from our husbands, Molly and I were being treated to a full day at San Diego's Sea World as participants in their Trainer for a Day program. We were both so excited it was all we could do to keep ourselves from leaping into the water instantly to play.

The morning lessons included a great deal of information on how the dolphins are trained and cared for. Wendy demonstrated a variety of tricks that our four dolphins already knew and she showed us how to use our whistles to reinforce successful behaviors. We then each had the opportunity to work with one of the dolphins—I worked with Malibu and Molly worked with Beaker. I first extended the flat of my hand toward Malibu, so that she would "target" me and I could establish eye contact with her. Then I gave her the signal to sing, which is wiggling my two index fingers, in response to which she promptly whistled and squeaked as she had earlier. As I did a circular motion with one hand, Malibu obediently responded with the "hula," which was really a pirouette with half her body sticking upright out of the water. I "danced" with her by kneeling on the ledge and holding her pectoral fins as she rose up in the water in front of me. Pointing somewhere with the index finger causes the dolphin to swim to that point, whereas pointing with the thumb (like a hitch-hiker) is the signal for going through the gate into the adjacent pool.

As we learned and executed the commands, Wendy explained that only positive reinforcement is given—never negative. If the animal doesn't do the correct action, or does something "bad," the trainer responds with Least Positive Scenario (LPS), which means giving no response except staying still and continuing to watch. After a pause, the command is repeated. The dolphins are never forced to respond to a command, nor are they forced to do a show— they only perform if and when they choose to.

As part of this morning session, we helped Wendy with the first round of food buckets. These are numbered and prepared for each animal, six times a day, with the food carefully weighed according to the plan posted on the board in the preparation area. The first round includes all of the vitamins and other medications prescribed for each animal. These pills are stuffed through a gill into the body of one of the biggest fish in each bucket and that fish is left on top, to be fed first. The food is a mix of mackerel, sardines, squid, and possibly other small fish. Wendy said that the park uses 2,000–3,000 pounds of fish each day. The food, of course, not only provides nourishment, but also acts as the primary reinforcement. Ice cubes are also apparently intrinsically reinforcing. Other "secondary" reinforcements include the whistle, applause, and verbal praise.

Following this pool session, Wendy took us into one of the back areas, where sick animals are quarantined and rescued animals are rehabilitated. Here we met Bodine, Sparky, Sandy, and Sydney. Sydney was a young bottlenose who had contracted a viral infection and was being quarantined. Because he was so young, his mother, Sandy, was with him. Sandy was also the mother of Diego, the other baby dolphin that I had seen in the show several years ago. Diego now lives at the Florida Sea World. Bodine and Sparky were sharing a pool with Nancy, a Pacific White-sided Dolphin—the only one of her kind at Sea World San Diego. All the other White-sided dolphins had been moved to Florida, but the staff had feared that Nancy was too old to make the move. However, that was 10 or 15 years ago and, surprisingly, she is still going strong. Although she has never had calves of her own (because of the lack of mates), she willingly acts as an "Auntie" to the young Bottlenose dolphins.

After practicing some of our commands with Bodine and Sparky, we talked with the trainer who was working this area and she showed us a tiny baby sea lion that had been rescued just two days previously. Its size indicated that it was hardly more than a newborn, but it had somehow become separated from its mother. The poor little thing looked very distressed and upset, crying and trying to crawl out of its enclosure through a far-too-narrow gap between the gate and fence. It seemed so lost and miserable and I felt so clumsy and useless as I watched it. It was a heart-wrenching moment and all I could do was wish that I could pick it up and comfort it. Fortunately, the Sea World staff are knowledgeable and well-equipped to handle such orphans, so this little one would at least have a fighting chance to survive and perhaps return to the wild.

We progressed then from the tiny to the titanic: stopping next at the Orca pool to meet Keet, Tara, and Kasatka. Kasatka was pregnant, due any day, so the trainers were calling her "Mom." Molly and I were assigned the task of peeling Orca-sized ice cubes: large paper soda cups filled with water and stored in the pool-side freezer. Not only are the ice cubes themselves used as rewards, the peeled scraps of paper cups become playthings, as one of the trainers demonstrated. She held a hand-sized scrap in her teeth and leaned out toward one of the Orcas, who gently took the scrap and then used her tongue to flip it back out of her mouth toward the trainer. The trainer then asked Keet to go and fetch a bucket, but after a long foray out into the depths of the pool, Keet returned without the bucket. It was Tara's turn next and the bucket she returned with was somewhat squashed and mangled: apparently the whales don't like the bucket very much. The trainer had "Mom" come close to the ledge, turning sideways to offer her huge left pectoral fin to us so that we could stroke her. Her skin glistened soft and smooth and as black as the Deep underneath my hand.

Another trainer called the three whales to the end of the pool and then sent one of them back to Molly who was instructed to lean over the water, splash her hand on the surface, and pull both hands up toward herself. This is the sign for "come here and spray me," which the whale promptly did. I got to do the same routine next, and received a whale-sized cold shower for my efforts. We observed a little while longer as the trainers played with all three Orcas, giving them more scraps of paper and having them pass chunks of ice cubes mouth-to-mouth from one whale to the next. It reminded me of a Halloween party game we used to play as kids—one person holds an apple under her chin and transfers it to the next person in line, without using any hands in the process. It was apparent to me that the whales enjoyed the ice cubes and the interactions with each other and their trainers. It was also clear that the trainers were strongly bonded to their charges and a feeling of wistful envy rose in me: how I wish that I had known such career choices existed when I was in college.

We sat at the tables next to the large Orca pool so that Wendy could give us our folders and go over some of the educational material while we relaxed and drank sodas, before heading back to the dolphin area. We showered and changed into dry clothes for our lunch break, which was very relaxing and peaceful. Since the table area was not open to the public for lunch, we had the whole place to ourselves. We sat quietly munching on our seafood salads as we watched the two Orcas swimming about and playing. The silence was broken periodically by their breathing—a very soothing and peaceful sound—and by the splashing and slapping of the water as the two raced, charged, dived, and generally cavorted, completely indifferent to our presence. All of their actions were spontaneous—there were no trainers interacting with them—and appeared relaxed and playful.

Down at the end of the pool we could see a trainer tending to a whale that Wendy had said was very sick with a lung infection. She had been placed in that area where there is a large shallow ledge, so that the trainers and vets could get to her quickly if needed. A large canopy had been strung overhead to keep her shaded. We watched a snowy egret daintily pick its way with yellow feet over the canopy and around the edge of the pool, as though it were a guardian angel on duty. As with the tiny baby sea lion, our hearts went out to this huge but fragile Orca, wishing her a speedy and complete recovery.

Wendy reappeared just as we finished our desserts. In answer to our questions, she said the big whale we had been observing with the Willy-like flopped-over dorsal fin is named Ulysses. She told us that there is always a 24-hour watch posted for the Orca pools. In part, this is for security reasons, but the primary purpose is to observe and record behavior, in order to increase our knowledge of these enormous mammals. All of the staff are involved in recording data for every animal that they train and care for: behaviors observed, progress (or difficulties) in training, what and how much the animals eat, the medications they are given, any signs of either physical or behavioral problems—all are meticulously recorded daily.

I was struck by the contrast between the experiences of these whales and that of Willy in the movie. These animals had all been born and raised in captivity, enjoying constant companionship, 24-hour care, and expert medical attention. Willy had been captured in the wild, torn from his mother's side when he was a baby, and had lived alone, with only a single trainer to care for him. Keiko's story was even worse: he was captured very young and had lived for 24 years in captivity, much of that without any other whales for companionship. For 11 years, he was kept in a small 12-foot deep tank in Mexico City. The conditions there were so bad that by the time he was moved, his health was very poor and his skin was covered with lesions.

Ulysses and his companion continued their leisurely cruising as Molly and I finished our whale-shaped cookies and followed Wendy to begin our afternoon's activities. Our first stop after lunch was the medical lab. The resident technician welcomed us and gave us a tour of the lab and operating room facilities. She explained with obvious pride and pleasure that both are very well equipped with the latest technology. Again, a strong wave of envy hit me and I wondered whether, had I known there were jobs such as this, I might have completed my original college major to become a medical technologist. Even after I changed my major to psychology, I could have gone to work at Sea World as a trainer. According to Wendy, the two best degrees to have are psychology or biology.

The technician took us into the spacious operating room, a cross between a hospital operating room and a very clean and tidy garage. She showed us x-rays and talked about some of the procedures that have been performed there, including setting a broken leg for a baby flamingo. The bones in the x-rays were thin and tiny and fragile looking and the photos showed a round fluff of a bird, not much larger than one of those bath sponges made from soft netting. The second set of x-rays revealed a dozen or more lead pellets embedded in the neck and head of a harbor seal that had been shot with a shotgun. My anger and outrage rose: I wanted to find the idiotic asshole who had done this and turn his own gun on him. Our guide said that the operating team had decided it would be more harmful to try to remove the pellets than to leave them in, that the animal had recovered, its wounds healing well, and that it was a permanent resident of Sea World now.

From the lab, Wendy took us to meet Gary, one of the sea lion trainers, and his two charges, Cheetah and Star. These two full grown sea lions were in training for tourist interaction duty at the Shipwreck Café. Gary needed "strangers" to help accustom the sea lions to being among and interacting with the general public, so he had enlisted the aid of the Trainer for a Day program to supply him with a steady (and more than willing) supply of strangers. As we walked back the short road to their enclosure, Cheetah and Star began leaping up and down at their gate, just like my German Shepherd or Molly's Australian Shepherd would do in anticipation of a walk. The two sea lions knew that they were going to be coming out for an excursion and they were clearly very eager to do so. Gary brought Cheetah out first and introduced her to Molly, letting Molly approach and pet her before returning her to the enclosure. This is a useful training exercise not only for the planned Café interactions, but also for those occasional visits by the vets, who are relative strangers to the animals.

Then Gary had me sit in the front passenger seat of the little open cart while he brought Star out and had her climb aboard the rear flatbed. She scrambled excitedly into, and then back out of, the cart precisely on command. On her next trip into the cart, Gary signaled her to rest her chin on the seat back, her face mere inches from my face, her big brown puppy eyes gazing directly into my eyes as her whiskers twitched with joy and enthusiasm. I grinned broadly at her in response, feeling her infectious joy welling up spontaneously inside me. With another trainer driving and Star riding in the back, rubber-necking the whole way, Gary and Molly and I walked ahead of the cart to keep strolling tourists from coming too close on our short trip over to the Café. On arrival, Gary put Star through her paces, having her go up on stage, stand at the podium, and pose for photos with Molly and me. Star was just as excited and cooperative on the ride back, and willingly obeyed Gary's commands to return to her enclosure. What a kick sea lions are—both Molly and I were struck by the parallels between these flippered fur-balls and their four-pawed counterparts who share our homes with us.

Now it was time for our afternoon pool sessions, so we returned to the locker room to change into wetsuits and booties (a fresh dry set—not the wet ones from the morning). We hurried over to Dolphin Stadium, where some of the other dolphin trainers welcomed us. Our first introduction was to Bubbles the Pilot whale, with whom we were able to pose side by side for photos. The trainers then introduced us to Bacardi, Malibu's mother. Bacardi is 14 years old and weighs about 630 pounds. Both Molly and I got to spend time in the water with her, doing the hula, a "flukes up" routine, a tandem back float, and then—best of all—riding around the pool on her back, hanging onto her dorsal fin. It was incredible to experience over 600 pounds of living muscular power beating beneath me as she pulled me through the water. Again the involuntary response—the laughter bubbled up and rushed through my throat to join the sparkling bow-wave along my forearms. I could no more have repressed that laughter than I could have walked on water.

We really didn't want this part of the day to end, but of course it had to and it was time for the Dolphin Show. We were introduced on stage at the beginning as the "Trainers for the Day" and we observed most of the show from behind the stage (we couldn't see much that way, unfortunately). When it was time, we went forward to help Wendy hold the long pole for Bubbles for her high jump. The sun glinted and danced on the agitated surface of the pool, making it difficult to see anything other than a large dark form as Bubbles moved to the far end, turned, and drove herself full speed toward the waiting pole. We gasped in amazement as she burst forth directly in front of us, soaring upward with the water cascading down her sleek blue-black sides. Her nose gently touched the float on the end of the pole, 15 feet above the surface, and then the pool exploded into a great geyser as she belly-flopped back down. In that instant I was a child again and I had just witnessed the most stupendous magical trick imaginable. The magic has remained with me since, playing over and over on an endless video loop in my mind, the immediacy and reality of it crowding out Willy's celluloid leap to freedom.

We finished the show as greeters standing on the rocks by the exit path as the audience left, saying good-bye to everyone, waving, inviting them to return. In spite of my natural shyness, I found myself actually enjoying this very unnatural role. I established eye contact with kids, adults—it didn't matter who—wished them well with genuine good will and bantered with ease, riding high on the wave of excitement that was rolling through and energizing me.

Still glowing and buzzing from the show, we returned to the dolphin interaction pools to observe and act as "spotters" for the afternoon DIP (Dolphin Interaction Program) session. There were four groups of four people participating, so all four of our dolphin friends from the morning were there: Misty, Beaker, Malibu and Bullet. "Spotting" the DIP means that we waited by the back pool to be with the dolphins if they were sent back by their trainer. We would keep them company (and play with them of course) until their trainer asked us to send them back out to the DIP pool, at which point we would give the "thumb" sign we had learned to direct them back through the gate. Malibu did a no-no during her DIP session: she swam around behind her group of participants. Although she didn't harm anyone, it is a potentially dangerous thing to do, so she was banished to the back pool for the remainder of the DIP. We were not allowed to interact with her in any way (sort of like our human practice of "time out" with a naughty child). I understood the necessity for that but it was a bit frustrating, as I really wanted more interaction with her.

The DIP ended about 3:45 and that signaled the end of our day as trainers. Neither Molly nor I wanted it to end. Again, the envy hit me. Wendy had told us about one man who signs up for the Trainer for a Day program once every month. Apparently, he is wealthy enough to be able to afford such a luxury and I knew that I would do the same if I had the money. Perhaps I can afford to do it once a year. I know that there are those who would consider such spending a frivolous waste. For me, it has not been frivolous, but an experience of deep joy that has energized me and expanded my universe immeasurably. There is no waste in that.

Since that day at Sea World, I have been using the Web to follow Keiko's story as it continues to unfold. The publicity from his movie debut resulted three years later in his being moved to a new custom-built tank in Oregon, where his improved living conditions combined with much-needed medical care brought him back to health. A carefully planned program began to train him to hunt and catch his own live food and in 1998 he was flown to a specially-built sea-pen in Iceland. A series of early attempts to free him from that pen failed because he did not bond with the wild Orcas nor did he leave the area, but in the summer of 2002, he finally began traveling and foraging with a wild pod.

Elation at this apparent progress turned to worry, however, when he arrived, alone, in Skaalvik Fjord in Norway in September of that year. Having spent all but 2 of his 24 years in captivity, and for many of those years with only humans as companions, Keiko apparently still prefers humans to whales for company. Having been fed by humans for most of his life, he apparently still assumed that they will feed him and he had stopped hunting. He spent much of his time with the throngs of humans who came to see him and he had become listless and exhausted. As of this writing (February 2003) he has been moved to another, more isolated location in Norway, where he is spending the winter. The Free Willy/Keiko Foundation intends to continue their efforts to reintroduce Keiko to the wild and maintains that the progress he has made so far has been extraordinary.

In the tradition of Hollywood, Willy made a magnificent leap over a breakwater to return to the open ocean—living happily ever after, as all would wish him to. But what will become of Keiko? At 24 years of age, he is nearing the end of his life. What does it mean for such an animal to live free before the wind? Is roaming the wild ocean automatically and unconditionally better than living in captivity? Where is the kindness, where is the justice, in forcing an individual to learn independence and a whole new way of life just as they are reaching their old age? Granted, he should not have been captured as a baby in the first place. However, I do not know the particulars of why that happened, so I cannot judge. He certainly should not have been isolated and mistreated in his early years. On the other hand, much of the treatment and care that he has received in the past decade has been humane and appropriate, competent and kind. But the fact remains that he has spent his whole life in captivity, in the company of humans, and now as he reaches old age we are denying him that contact and expecting him to want to fend for himself.

Are whales and dolphins capable of feeling happiness and sorrow, of establishing emotional bonds with other beings? Do they feel the pain of loneliness? I believe that they do. Dr. Candace Pert, a pioneering researcher in the field of neuroimmunology, points out in her book, *Molecules of Emotion*, that the limbic system of the brain, long considered the "seat of emotions," is very rich in receptors not only for pleasure-producing opiates but also for many other neuropeptide chemicals which are associated with a wide range of emotions. She goes on to state that, "In fact, the receptor-mapping experiments I'd done... had shown that identical opiate receptors could be found in the brains of all vertebrates, from the simple, hideous hagfish to the complex, exalted human. Even insects and other invertebrates could be shown to have opiate receptors."

So even though the perpetual grin of the dolphin is merely an artifact of mouth shape, this does not negate the notion that these highly intelligent mammals are, very much like humans, a complex mixture of intelligence and emotion. Those who attribute such traits to mammals other than humans have long been accused of "anthropomorphizing" and living in a fantasy world, but current research indicates clearly that it is those who insist on the uniqueness and separateness of humans who are living the fantasy. We humans are inextricably bound with these great ocean-dwelling mammals and owe them the same respect and love that we owe to each other.

Does that obligation mean that we should expect Keiko to return to an ocean wilderness that he has never known? Does it mean that we should not keep any of these creatures captive in our zoos and aquariums? Does it mean, as some animal rights activists have proposed, that we should prohibit all contact between us and these other beings, lest they be changed by their interactions with us? This is not Hollywood and there are no simple answers to these questions. There are no "one-size-fits-all" solutions. Both in the wild and in captivity, it is clear that animals do change their behavior based on interactions with humans. They learn to trust or to fear, they learn to depend or to flee, they bond or they avoid, based on our human actions. What is equally clear is that we humans also change because of these interactions. We increase our knowledge, we experience profound joy and sadness, and we continually search for ways in which we can expand our community to include these extraordinary beings. Hopefully, our research will help us to learn how to care for them better, cure their illnesses, and prevent needless deaths. Hopefully, in some small way we can contribute to their well-being and survival, both as individuals and as species, both in captivity and in the wild. Perhaps in the process we will even be smart enough and sensitive enough to learn the one great secret that they possess: the knowledge of how to live always before the wind.

Epilogue: Europe at 75

*"The real voyage of discovery consists not in
seeing new landscapes but in having new eyes."*
— *Marcel Proust*

By early 1992, we had accrued enough vacation days and frequent flier miles, and advanced far enough up the pay scale, that we were ready to plan a major vacation. The question was: Where should we go? Neither of us had ever been to Europe and we love French wine and Italian opera, so Europe was a serious candidate. Then a friend of ours told us about her diving experiences in Borneo and that made our decision for us. Off to Borneo we went. We were both 46 at the time, so we made a pact with each other: Unless we managed to strike it rich somehow, we would keep choosing diving vacations as long as we were physically able to dive.

The real significance of our little pact wasn't apparent to us until halfway through our week of diving in Borneo. We were sitting on the dock one evening, sipping our gin and tonics and chatting with two of the couples we had been diving with. We were very surprised to learn that all four of them were in their late 60s or early 70s, retired, and doing one or two dive trips a year. One of the wives told us her harrowing tale of being stranded on the surface, out of air, with her companions still underwater and the dive boat very far away, as a 10-foot tiger shark circled repeatedly around her. Someone who would keep diving after such an experience was certainly not going to let a little thing like old age deter her from diving. This was when we realized the implications of our pact; if we were lucky, we wouldn't make it to Europe until we were in our mid-70s. And so, we honed our pact into a private battle cry: Europe at 75—and not before!

In recent years, we've "cheated" a bit. Jon has been to London twice on business trips and I recently accompanied him to Paris for a week while he attended a technical conference. Nevertheless, our basic resolve remains: We will keep diving until we are no longer physically able to do so. Who can say how long that will be? For both of us, our genetic heritage has handed us some lemons; Jon's arthritis is persistent, slowly but inexorably misshaping and fusing his spine, while I struggle constantly to prevent my misguided immune system from sapping my energy and destroying more of my body's substance. Ruefully we joke about how remarkably well-matched we are: he is always in pain and I am always tired. We'll both be 57 this year and we have certainly slowed down quite a bit. We no longer do two local boat dives a month—only three or four a year now. We can't do four or five dives in a day as our younger friends can—we're happy to be able to do two or three.

Yes, we are slowing down, but we're not even close to quitting yet. One of our friends gave up cold-water diving after his 75th birthday but continued doing warm-water diving for several years after that. The July/August 2000 issue of Alert Diver printed an article about Jane Woodward, a grandmother who began diving at the age of 72 and was still diving at 79. As for physical handicaps, we have had the privilege of diving with one man who had had his right leg amputated just below the knee, and another man who was permanently paralyzed from mid-chest down. With examples like these to inspire us, we do everything in our power to stay as physically fit as possible, and continue to dive as often as we can.

In the 30 years that I have been diving I have logged close to 1,000 dives, but that is not nearly enough. The magic and adventure of that other universe under the sea continue to speak to me. From the moment I first looked beneath the surface, I have suffered a sea change. My very existence has been enriched beyond measure by the hours I have spent in the ocean. Because I can experience that other three-fourths of our planet, my world is four times larger than if I had remained landlocked. Diving has taught me to slow down and focus and to simply be—to see and become a part of the wild beauty that engulfs me. And so, I return again and again. I cannot imagine ever growing tired of making that journey.

Epitaph

Smoke embraces sky
Ashes seek the ocean's depth
I merge into Blue.